Also by Ellen M. Kozak

From Pen to Print:
The Secrets of Getting Published Successfully

Every Writer's Guide
to Copyright
and Publishing Law

EVERY WRITER'S GUIDE TO

©OPYRIGHT AND

PUBLISHING LAW

THIRD EDITION

ELLEN M. KOZAK

AN OWL BOOK

HENRY HOLT AND COMPANY • NEW YORK

Owl Books
Henry Holt and Company, LLC
Publishers since 1866
175 Fifth Avenue
New York, New York 10010
www.henryholt.com

Distributed in Canada by H. B. Fenn and Company Ltd.

Library of Congress Cataloging-in-Publication Data

Kozak, Ellen M.
    Every writer's guide to copyright and publishing law /
Ellen M. Kozak.—3rd ed.
        p.   cm.
    Includes index.
    ISBN-13: 978-0-8050-7378-2
    ISBN-10: 0-8050-7378-7
        1. Copyright—United States—Popular works.   2. Authors
and publishers—United States—Popular works.   I. Title.

KF3020.Z9K685   2004
346.7304'82—dc22

                                            2003056808

Henry Holt books are available for special promotions
and premiums. For details contact: Director, Special Markets.

First Edition 1990
Third Edition 2004
Designed by Victoria Hartman

Printed in the United States of America

10   9   8   7   6   5   4   3   2

The information in this book is provided as a source of general
information only, and is not intended as legal advice or opinion.
For specific information applying to a particular matter, readers
should contact a licensed attorney who practices in this area of law.

*For Mom and Dad
and Josh and Seth
and Claire Rose*

Contents

Acknowledgments

For the first edition:

A circle of supportive friends and family make a book possible; so it is with this one—I couldn't have managed without my parents, sisters, brother, agent, dog, and friends too numerous to mention. But there are some who deserve specific mention because of their specific involvement with *this* volume.

This book grew out of a booklet that grew out of my column in *The Inkling* (later known as *Writer's Journal*), a magazine that was edited, published, incubated, and nursed along by my dedicated and very decent friend John Hall, who, like me, has since left the publication. The earliest columns antedated my entry into the computer age and were "word processed on the typewriter and the copier" by Nada Vuckovic Cosic; later columns and the manuscript for this book, composed on the computer, were copied and cataloged by Barbara Riedel. Each of these women has been, in turn, my mainstay in my law practice and my writing career; both of them have also become my very good friends.

Christina Lucchesi's research assistance proved both timely and invaluable. Tracy Bernstein was a patient and supportive editor. Special thanks go to attorney Bardin Levavy, Professor Ramon Klitzke of the Marquette University Law School, U.S. Bankruptcy Court judge Margaret Dee McGarity, and the United States Copyright Office for their helpful input. My gratitude, too, to Mary Mahoney of the Marquette University Law Library and to attorneys Diana Rich Segal and Evelyn Subotky for coming through when the chips were down.

And I would be remiss if I didn't mention the late Alan Latman, professor of law at New York University and executive director of the Copyright Society of the U.S.A., a dedicated scholar and wonderful teacher whose presence in the copyright community is sorely missed.

Ellen M. Kozak

Milwaukee, Wisconsin
April 1, 1990

For the second edition:

More of the same—with special thanks to a *very patient* Tracy Sherrod, my editor and fellow dog lover; to attorney Howard Zaharoff and Canadian barrister and solicitor Margaret Ann Wilkinson for their friendship and counsel; and to Scooter and Shade for their boon companionship.

EMK

Milwaukee, Wisconsin
October 1996

For the third edition:

Still more of the same, and thanks to an even more patient Deb Brody, to Aileen for helping get the place in order, and to Muffin and Sparky for behaving (occasionally).

EMK

Milwaukee, Wisconsin
November 2003

Every Writer's Guide
to Copyright
and Publishing Law

1.

Ground Rules

Whether it is beans, diamonds, or sedans, farmers, jewelers, and car dealers generally know precisely what they are selling. And while the identity of the actual product becomes a bit blurred in the service industries—a travel agent sells you her expertise in addition to your airplane ticket, a barber his artistic finesse in addition to your haircut—in the end, you come away with a concrete product you can call your own: the ticket, the haircut.

But common terminology fails in the publishing world. When you tell people you've "sold" your book, you normally don't mean that you've gone out on the street corner and peddled a copy; you mean that you've convinced a publisher to pay you money for the right to print copies, which he or she will then (usually with a few middlemen in between) sell to the public.

Just what have you sold when you sell your writing to a publisher or producer? Most writers haven't a clue that what is for sale is an intangible: the *rights* you have in your work.

This book is designed to help you understand the sale of such rights and the responsibilities that go with such a sale. The law that applies to this is generally *copyright* law, although other areas, such as *trademark, contract, agency, libel, privacy,* and *tax* law may also be involved.

These are matters that you, as a writer, should make it your business to understand, because, unfortunately, if you give away too many rights, or infringe on someone else's rights through your writing, it does you no good to plead ignorance of the law. While you may not go to jail, you *may* find yourself at a financial disadvantage—unable to collect money you should have received or paying substantial amounts for legal fees or even for restitution to others.

Writers seldom have much grounding in the legal aspect of writing, but then, few lawyers have much grounding in it either. Although this is changing as copyright law's importance in the electronic age is being acknowledged, few law schools have traditionally offered courses in copyright law, generally preferring to combine it with classes in patent and trademark law where copyrights often come off a poor third. And even when copyright courses are available, not many law students have taken them. Thus your family lawyer may not be able to help you out when you have a copyright problem and may not be familiar enough with the customs of the trade to help you out with a publishing contract. This book is designed to give you enough grounding in this esoteric area of law to know when to seek professional help, but before I let you in on any of these secrets, let me lay down a few ground rules.

RULE 1 is that this book is designed to cover *U.S. law* as it pertains to writing and writers' rights. While the United States is bound by a number of treaties to protect the copyrights in works that originate in many other countries, there are exceptions and variations that are too numerous to go into in this volume. Although some material on international copyright applications is provided in chapter 16, if you are a Turkish citizen whose book was first published in Bulgaria and your habitual residence is Beijing, the information in this book may not apply to you. See a copyright lawyer to find out what law *does*.

RULE 2 is that this book is meant only to be a *guide* to *general principles* of law. It isn't meant to turn you into a lawyer; even three years of law school doesn't always do that. So keep in mind that a little knowledge can be a dangerous thing. See a copyright lawyer (or at least check with the Copyright Office) if you aren't sure if a general principle presented here applies to *your* case.

RULE 3 is that the *law can change*. This can happen in two ways. First, the wording of the law itself can and does change when new laws are passed (after all, members of Congress have to do something to earn their salaries). And second, the meaning of the words in a law can change when judges interpret sections of the law that parties to a lawsuit have found to be ambiguous (this is what keeps lawyers in business).

Thus, although every effort has been made to make sure this book is as current as possible, a judge whose breakfast isn't sitting well or a member of Congress who tacks the right amendment onto the wrong bill can render even the most longstanding principle obsolete. Lawyers routinely read "advance sheets" and attend seminars in order to keep current on new developments in the law, so again, you may want to double-check with the Copyright Office (which can advise you about filing, but cannot give specific legal advice) or with a publishing attorney, just to make sure the law is still the same.

RULE 4 is that *unique circumstances may cause your case to be the exception* to any general rule presented here. Each case is ultimately determined by its specific facts. Again, checking with a copyright lawyer or with the Copyright Office can help you determine if your case is an exception. And bear in mind that responsibility for complying with the law rests ultimately with you.

RULE 5 is that *this book is primarily concerned with literary works*. If you are involved with other types of copyrightable material—if, for example, you write music or movies, design buildings or computer programs, or if you have an interest in the recording of a performance—although I've tried to touch on these areas, some exceptions to the information in this book may apply. Again, check with the Copyright Office or with an attorney to make sure what your rights and responsibilities may be.

In other words, this book is meant to give you a general understanding of the way publishing law works, but it is not meant to supplant the advice of a competent professional. It can, however, save you money when you do seek professional advice by helping you to zero in on problems: lawyers generally bill by the hour, so getting to the point can save you time *and* money.

2.

Publishing Law and the Legal System

Before you can understand how copyright and the other laws that apply to publishing operate, you need to understand how the American legal system works.

In the United States, only *some* of the laws are "on the books" as the result of legislative drafting. The rest of our law is based on precedent—the rulings of judges in previous cases. A judge may extrapolate from the decisions of other courts in similar matters, or may rely on throwaway lines of reasoning (known as *dicta*) found in totally unrelated cases. Sometimes (when such information is available) a decision is reached by looking at the legislative history of a law and trying to determine from amendments to its original form and from the content of legislative arguments what the drafters of the law meant by the wording they chose.

And sometimes a judge merely takes his or her best guess at what the words must mean or how they should be applied to the facts of your case. Whichever pattern the court follows, when the resulting decision is the only one on the subject, a new law has been created. A precedent established by the decision of a court is as valid as a statute, though it may not be as precise, and may be more difficult to locate.

Adding to the confusion this creates is the fact that courts of equal jurisdiction do not have to abide by each other's rulings. (A court's jurisdiction is its scope of authority.) In the United States, there are two separate and essentially independent court systems, federal and state—and each state's courts are unique and independent from those of every other state. Generally, cases involving violations of state laws and lawsuits between persons living in the same state are brought in the state courts. Cases concerning U.S. law (including constitutional issues) and cases between citizens of different states (if they involve large enough sums) can originate in the federal courts.

Copyrights are authorized by the U.S. Constitution, and the complete revision of the U.S. Copyright Law enacted in 1976 preempted all state laws regarding copyrights. This means that copyrights are governed only by federal law, and that copyright matters may be brought *only* in the *federal* courts. (However, related matters, such as plagiarism, libel, or disputes over publishing contracts that do not involve copyright matters normally belong in the state courts.) And in some instances where a copyright issue is introduced into a case after the initial complaint, the case may remain in the state court system.

Under the federal court system, each state has at least one district court, although some states, depending on their population, are divided into several judicial districts. All district courts in the United States technically have equal jurisdiction and need not follow each other's rulings, although as a matter of practicality they often do so.

The district courts' rulings can be appealed to the appropriate court of appeals for one of the eleven numbered federal circuits (so named because their judges used to "ride the circuit" from one district court to another) or the District of Columbia Circuit. The jurisdiction of each numbered federal circuit incorporates the district courts of several states. A ruling from a circuit court of appeals is generally binding on all of the district courts within its circuit, but it does not bind other circuit or district courts, although they may follow it if they so choose.

If you are dissatisfied with the decision of a circuit court of appeals, you can appeal to the U.S. Supreme Court. If the Supreme Court accepts the case, its decision is binding on all the courts in the nation. (When it declines to rule on a case presented to it, such inaction is often interpreted as tacit approval of the lower court's stance, although the Supreme Court may have had other reasons for refusing the case. This may result in broader application of an appeals court ruling than would otherwise be the case.)

There is yet another way to divide the U.S. court system: both state and federal courts have different rules for civil and criminal cases. *Criminal* proceedings are brought by the government against those who break its rules, from running a stoplight to failing to pay taxes to committing murder. A *civil* case normally does not involve the government, being instead a dispute between two or more people (or corporations, since a corporation is an "artificial person" for the purpose of litigation). There are four real differences between civil and criminal matters: who brings the suit, what is at stake, who gets any awards, and who bears the burden of proof.

A civil suit can be initiated by any aggrieved party; however, a criminal case must be brought by a prosecutor who represents the government. What is at stake in a criminal matter may be your liberty, since a verdict of "guilty" can result in a jail sentence as well as a fine. In a civil case, the issue is usually money, although a ruling may also involve an "equitable" remedy such as an *injunction*—in copyright matters, this might be an order to cease and desist from distributing infringing materials. In copyright matters, courts also have the authority to order the destruction of infringing goods.

Then there's the matter of who gets the money. In a criminal case, if a fine is levied, the money goes to the state, *not* to the injured party (although sometimes restitution is ordered as a condition of probation or of a suspended sentence). In a civil matter, the losing side normally compensates the other party for its damages and may have to pay the other side's legal fees as well. The most familiar example of this difference is probably that of an automobile accident: You can be fined for going through a red light, but the owner of the car you then hit will not be compensated out of that fine for injuries or damage. To obtain compensation (unless a settlement between the parties can be reached), he or she must bring a civil suit.

The final difference between civil and criminal matters is the burden of proof. In a civil case, the plaintiff usually needs to establish only that a preponderance of the evidence is in his favor; in a criminal matter, the prosecutor must satisfy the judge and jury that the defendant is guilty beyond a reasonable doubt—a higher standard that is usually more difficult to attain.

Just as it is possible to find yourself facing both a criminal action (e.g., a traffic citation) and a civil one (a suit for injuries to the person and damages to the vehicle you hit) as a result of the same automobile accident, you can find yourself faced with both civil and criminal liability in a copyright matter. But because the standards of proof are so high, and because federal prosecutors are busy prosecuting bank robbers, tax evaders, terrorists, and drug pushers, criminal copyright proceedings are initiated less frequently than civil proceedings. Though civil cases are more common, they can be just as expensive to try—and if you lose, you can be ordered to pay the other side's legal fees as well as your own. Thus it is a much better strategy to protect yourself in advance than to resolve problems in the courts.

3.

Definitions

Before we proceed further, it might help for you to familiarize yourself with the basic vocabulary of copyright and publishing law. Here are some of the more common terms.

All rights. This means all the rights that may exist in a creative work. When you assign all rights, you are essentially assigning the copyright in that work and may even be giving away more (see the discussion of moral rights in chapter 14).

Anonymous work. As defined in the U.S. Copyright Law, this is a work in which "no natural person is identified as author" on the copies or phonorecords on which the work is reproduced.

Author. While this term is not found among the definitions in the U.S. Copyright Law, it generally means the creator (or creators) of a work, except in the case of a work made for hire, in which case it means the employer or commissioning party (see chapter 5).

Berne Convention. The Berne Convention for the Protection of Literary and Artistic Works is an international copyright treaty first signed at Berne, Switzerland, on September 9, 1886. The United States became a member of the community of nations that have signed this treaty as of March 1, 1989.

Book rights. The right to publish a work in book form. These rights can be subdivided by geography (e.g., North American book rights), by language (English-language book rights), or by type of book (hardcover, trade paperback, or mass market paperback). Some recent case law has distinguished between e-books and printed ones, so this term may not be as obvious as it seems.

Collective work. As defined in the U.S. Copyright Law, this is "a work, such as a periodical issue, anthology, or encyclopedia, in which a number of contributions, constituting separate and independent works in themselves, are assembled into a collective whole."

Compilation. A work formed by collecting and assembling preexisting materials or data "in such a way that the resulting work as a whole constitutes an original work of authorship" based on the way it is "selected, coordinated, or arranged." The U.S. Copyright Law goes on to say that "the term 'compilation' includes collective works."

Contract. An agreement between two or more parties that can be enforced in court. Sometimes this term is used to refer to the written document on which the agreement of the parties is recorded (see chapter 13).

Copyright. This term is not defined in the text of the U.S. Copyright Law, although the law does define its parameters. Generally, a copyright is the name given to the "bundle of rights" that exists in a work that qualifies for protection under copyright law.

Copyright law. The body of law that governs the exploitation of literary, musical, artistic, and related works. It governs computer programs because they are considered to be literary works. It also covers audio, visual, and audiovisual works, and even the performances embodied in such works. In the United States, the Copyright Law is contained in Title 17 of the U.S. Code, in combination with the regulations of the Copyright Office and the cases that have interpreted Title 17 and those regulations.

Copyright Office. Copyright records and registrations are administered by the Copyright Office under the direction of the Register of Copyrights. The Copyright Office is part of the Library of Congress and is therefore part of the federal government. It is located in the Madison Building of the Library of Congress, and is open to the public weekdays except for federal holidays. Its mailing address is: Library of Congress, Copyright Office, 101 Independence Avenue, S.E., Washington, D.C. 20559-6000. (See chapter 23 for security regulations that now apply to submissions and to visiting the Copyright Office in person.)

Derivative work. As defined in the U.S. Copyright Law, this is "a work based upon one or more preexisting works, such as a translation, musical arrangement, dramatization, fictionalization, motion picture version, sound recording, art reproduction, abridgement, condensation, or any other form in which a work may be recast, transformed, or adapted. A work consisting of editorial revisions, annotations, elaborations, or other modifications, which, as a whole, represents an original work of authorship, is a 'derivative work.'" Sequels and prequels are also derivative works.

Joint work. This is a work created by two or more authors with the intent that their work "be merged into inseparable or interdependent parts of a unitary whole." This intent must be present when each party creates his or her portion of the work; adding to an already existing work creates a derivative, rather than a joint, work. Note also the differences between a "joint work," a "supplementary work," and a "collective work."

Pseudonymous work. From "pseudonym," this is a work in which "the author is identified under a fictitious name" on the copies or phonorecords in which the work is reproduced.

Publication. This term as defined in the text of the U.S. Copyright Law means the distribution of copies of a work to the public "by sale or other transfer of ownership" (this could include gifts and donations) "or by rental, lease or lending. The offering to distribute copies" can constitute publication, but a public performance or display of a work normally does not.

Registration. A work can be registered with the Copyright Office. Such registration may offer added protection but normally is not a prerequisite for the establishment of copyright, although a U.S. work must be registered before you can bring suit for its infringement, and prompt registration can result in certain extra protections and benefits (see chapters 10 and 22).

Serial rights. These are the rights to publish a work in a "serial" publication, such as a magazine or newspaper.

Subsidiary rights. A publishing term not mentioned in the U.S. Copyright Law although protected by it, subsidiary rights are generally the nonbook rights contained in a book contract. They can include derivative rights, such as dramatization, adaptation, or translation, and ancillary rights, such as publication in other media (for example, serialization or audio recording). These rights are sometimes designated as ancillary rights.

Work for hire (also "work made for hire"). A work in which all rights belong to the commissioning party or employer if certain conditions are met (see chapter 5).

4.

"Intellectual Property"—Copyrights, Patents, and Trademarks

The United States Constitution, in Article I, section 8, grants Congress the power "to promote the Progress of Science and useful Arts, by securing for limited Times to Authors and Inventors the exclusive Right to their respective Writings and Discoveries." This is the legal basis for America's patent and copyright laws, the first of which were passed in 1790.

Inventions and discoveries (such as gene sequences), methods, and procedures, when they qualify, can be eligible for *patent* protection. If you're interested in obtaining a patent, see a patent attorney; patent law is a recognized legal specialty and lawyers who practice in the Patent Office must pass a special exam to do so.

Among the categories of works that can be protected by *copyright* are music, art (including maps, photographs, sculpture, technical drawings, and architectural plans), literature, dramas, motion pictures and other audiovisual works, pantomimes and choreography, and sound recordings. Computer programs are also eligible for copyright protection, as are architectural works (yes, houses and other buildings, as well as their blueprints, are protectable!). Performances can be protected as well, if they are recorded. No special exams are required to practice in this area of law, but since few law schools have traditionally offered courses in the subject and even fewer law students take them, expertise in this area is normally obtained by experience in the field. Comparatively few legal practitioners handle copyright matters; fewer still are knowledgeable about the specific customs of businesses such as music, art, or publishing, which are often distinct from one another.

Trademark law covers the use of product names and logos. Trademarks can be registered in the U.S. Patent and Trademark Office when they qualify for federal protection, but this protection is based on the section of the Constitution that allows the federal government to regulate interstate commerce, not on the section that mandates patent and copyright laws. Trademarks and trade names used exclusively within a single state are usually regulated by the laws of that state. Thus it is possible for a person or company to hold a valid trademark within a single state that is the same as a valid trademark in use solely within the borders of another state; it is generally only when one of these users expands his business or affects commerce beyond the borders of his or her home state that federal law comes into play.

Other areas of law, such as *trade secrets* and *unfair competition*, are often included within the category of intellectual property law as well. Unless they fall within the purview of federal trademark laws, they are generally governed by state law.

Patents and copyrights, since they are authorized by the Constitution, are governed by federal law. This law is the same throughout the United States, although its interpretation may vary from jurisdiction to jurisdiction. The major revision of the U.S. Copyright Law that took effect on January 1, 1978, pre-empts all state authority in matters covered by federal copyright law; this means all works of sufficient length (there is no copyright in a name or a short phrase) are covered by federal law once they have been fixed in a medium of expression from which they can be read back. (There is no copyright protection for facts or ideas; it is the way the facts are assembled, or the expression of the idea, that is protected.)

The copyright law revision that took effect on January 1, 1978, is known as "the 1976 law," because that was the year it was enacted. It is also frequently referred to as the "new law" to distinguish it from the previous law, which is generally referred to as "the 1909 law," or the "old law."

The 1976 law underwent considerable modification as of March 1, 1989, when the United States joined the Berne Convention for the Protection of Literary and Artistic Works. The modifications to U.S. copyright law that were required for U.S. membership in the Berne were contained in the Berne Convention Implementation Act of 1988, otherwise known as the BCIA.

Other major reforms, such as the Copyright Renewal Act of 1992 (the CRA), the changes brought about by U.S. ratification of the North American Free Trade Agreement (NAFTA) in 1993, and the General Agreement on Tariffs and Trade (the GATT) in 1994, have also altered U.S. copyright law, and further reforms are pending in Congress.

The Digital Millennium Copyright Act (DMCA) of 1998, the Sonny Bono Copyright Term Extension Act of that same year, and the Technology, Education, and Copyright Harmonization

(TEACH) Act of 2002 are just some of the laws Congress has passed to keep up with technological and global market changes.

The practical effect of these changes is that there are different sets of rules that can apply to a copyrightable work. The governing factor in determining which rules apply to a given work is usually the *date of its first publication*. Thus:

> Notice on and transfer of copyright for works *first published before January 1, 1978*, are governed by the 1909 law (as modified by the provisions of the 1976 law that extended the renewal term and the Sonny Bono law that extended it yet again). The need to renew the copyright in such works depends on whether they were *first published before or after January 1, 1964* (because of the CRA's automatic renewal provisions), and whether they qualify for recapture under NAFTA or the GATT.
>
> The copyright in a work *first published between January 1, 1978, and February 28, 1989*, is governed by the 1976 law in its original form (requiring copyright notice) except that works subject to recapture under NAFTA and the GATT did not permanently lose their copyrights for failing to comply with formalities (such as the notice requirement) then in effect. But the duration of these copyrights was extended by the Sonny Bono Act as well.
>
> The copyright in a work *first published on or after March 1, 1989*, comes under the rules of the 1976 law as modified by the BCIA (and by the CRA and the Sonny Bono Act). As there were no formalities required for copyright protection in the United States after that date, foreign copyrights were not lost for lack of compliance; therefore the subject of U.S. copyright restoration for them is moot.

From this, you should be able to see that to ascertain the copyright status of a work, the two most important questions you can ask yourself are, "Has the work been published?" and, if so, "When was it published?" The answers to those questions will generally tell you which law applies. A further question, "Is the work of non-U.S. origin," may be helpful in determining whether the modifications resulting from U.S. ratification of NAFTA or the GATT may apply to it. If so, further research into its copyright status may be necessary.

5.

Copyright Origins and Duration

Under United States law, copyright protection exists in an original work from the moment it is fixed in a tangible medium of expression from which it can be read back either directly or by electronic, mechanical, or any other means. Incomplete works as well as completed ones and all revisions of a work can be protected. The minute you preserve the work in some form that can be read back, you own the copyright in it; basically, copyright ownership is that simple.

To fix the work, you can write it, type it, dictate it to a secretary who takes it down in shorthand or on a court reporting machine, recite it into a tape recorder, act it out in front of a video camera, or carve it in clay, wax, or stone. Once you've created and fixed the work, the copyright exists—provided the work is *original*.

What does it take for a work to be original? The Supreme Court has ruled that a mere alphabetical listing of telephone numbers does not have the requisite creative spark, no matter how much time and effort went into compiling that list. For other types of writing, however, the definition is not so simple.

Obviously, there is nothing new under the sun, and the courts recognize that there may be a limited number of basic plots—but it is how you develop a plot that makes it original. Unlike patents, copyrights do not require that a work be *novel*—that is, unlike anything ever created before—and no search of previously copyrighted materials need be made. Indeed, some plot devices are accepted as generic and may be incorporated into any work; called *scènes à faire*, these include generic elements such as cowboys wearing spurs, armies carrying weapons, and scientists working in laboratories.

The key to originality is that you must have created your work without copying or having access to any other work to which it is substantially similar. Thus, if you pound out your novel on a typewriter in your attic in Maine while someone else is scribbling an almost identical book on notepads on the beach in California but neither of you has had access to the other's work, each of you will own the copyright in your own creation and may exploit it fully.

This may not hold true if one of the books has been published and distributed widely before the other is created. Even if you never saw the other writer's published work, there is case law to suggest that your access to it will be presumed. In law, a *presumption* is accepted as true unless you can prove it to the contrary. If you can prove that you were locked in a cave during the entire period that the other book was on the best-seller lists, you might be able to establish that your work was indeed original. Otherwise, where there are too many similarities and access was *possible*, the court will usually assume there was copying.

However, once your work qualifies as original and has been fixed in any tangible medium of expression, it is protected by copyright. Under current law, copyright protection for such works—if they remained unpublished as of January 1, 1978, or were created after that date—generally exists for the life of the author plus seventy years, and the copyrights belong to the author until he or she signs or gives them away.

Works that were first published before January 1, 1978, could be protected for a term of twenty-eight years from their first publication under the 1909 law. A single renewal of twenty-eight years made it possible to extend copyright protection for a total of fifty-six years. However, if the copyright wasn't renewed, the work fell into the public domain at the end of the first twenty-eight years. *A work first published as recently as December 31, 1964, must have been renewed by the end of the twenty-eighth year after its first publication or its copyright lapsed.* However, many *foreign* works that lost their U.S. copyright protection for failure to comply with formalities such as renewals were *restored* when the United States ratified the GATT, and now endure for as long as they would have had their copyrights not been lost (see below).

The 1976 law extended the renewal term for works published before January 1, 1978, to forty-seven years instead of twenty-eight, for a total of seventy-five years instead of fifty-six, but this applied only to works still protected by copyright on that date. Certain exceptions were made for works that would otherwise have entered the public domain during the period Congress was debating the 1976 revisions, but if a work did not qualify for one of these exceptions, or if it had already entered the public domain, the extension did not apply.

The Copyright Renewal Act of 1992 eliminated the necessity of making formal renewal of pre-1978 works in order to gain the additional forty-seven years. However, since this act was not retroactive, automatic renewals apply only to works first published since January 1, 1964. The copyright term for works first published between that date and December 31, 1977, was seventy-five years, but renewal in the twenty-eighth year can affect the ownership of certain rights during the remainder of the copyright (see chapter 11 for more on this).

The renewal term was extended for an additional twenty years as a result of the Sonny Bono Act of 1998. But works that reached their seventy-fifth year in 1997 fell into the public domain under the previous law, and for *U.S.* copyrights, once a work is in the public domain, it remains there. Thus U.S. works first published in 1922 are in the public domain, but those first published in 1923 will be protected through 2018.

The "life-plus-fifty-years" rule that generally applied to works unpublished on or created after January 1, 1978, became "life plus seventy" with the passage of the Bono Act. But there are three exceptions. Anonymous works, pseudonymous works, and works made for hire enjoy copyright protection for 120 years from their creation or ninety-five years from their first publication, whichever is sooner. You can change this to life-plus-seventy status in the case of anonymous and pseudonymous works if you inform the Copyright Office that you are in fact the author. However, works that fall validly into the work-made-for-hire classification remain there, and their term of copyright protection cannot be altered.

Where non-U.S. works are concerned, you may want to check with the Copyright Office because the old rule that once a work fell into the public domain it remained there has been changed by the U.S. ratification of NAFTA and the GATT.

Under those treaties, a mechanism was put into place for the protection of U.S. copyrights for certain foreign works that had fallen into the public domain in the United States (but not in their country of origin) for failure to comply with American formalities in effect at the time. Only works originating in countries *other* than the United States were affected by this change; copyrights in U.S. works cannot be recaptured. Copyrights in all such works originating in other World Trade Organization (WTO) countries, if they were less than seventy-five years old and were still protected in their country of origin, were automatically reinstated when the GATT took effect in the United States, and NAFTA did this for some North American works. And with the passage of the Bono Act, twenty more years have been added to their copyright term.

As I mentioned earlier, copyright normally belongs to the *creator* of a work from the moment it is fixed. Works made for hire are the exception—where there is a *valid* work for hire, the person or corporation who hired you to create the work is the "author" for copyright purposes and owns the copyright. The key word here is "valid." The abuses of the work-for-hire section of the law remind me of the old joke that asks, "If you call its tail a leg, how many legs does a sheep have?" The answer is four—calling a tail a leg doesn't make it one, and saying something is a work made for hire doesn't necessarily mean it is one, either.

Preparing a work on an assigned or commissioned basis does not automatically make it a work for hire. There are only two ways a work can fall into the work-for-hire classification. One is when it is created by an employee within the scope of his or her employment. Unfortunately, the U.S. Copyright Law neglected to define "employee" or "employment," so it fell to the Supreme Court to do so.

The Supreme Court suggested that the guidelines set forth in another area of the law, agency law, must be considered in order to determine who can be designated as an employee. Under that law, the basis for the establishment of an employment relationship is the hiring party's right to control the "manner and means by which the product is accomplished." In sum, this requires an analysis of who controls where the work is done, at what times, and with whose tools. Other factors that must also be considered include the skill required to create the work, the duration of the relationship between the parties, the method of payment, and whether employee benefits are provided and normal deductions withheld. Also to be considered are each party's role in hiring and paying assistants, and whether the hiring party has the right to assign additional projects to the hired party.

If the consideration of such factors does not, cumulatively, convince the court that an employment relationship exists, you are not an employee, and the work you have created is not made for hire. However, the Supreme Court declined to rule that "employee" meant "formal, salaried employee" (although most courts have interpreted it that way), so it is possible that the product of a volunteer's labor could be considered work made for hire.

Again, even where you *are* found to be an employee, the work must be performed within the scope of your employment to fall within this classification. Thus news articles written by a newspaper reporter are works made for hire, but a novel he or she writes on his or her own time is not, nor is ad copy written by a receptionist if the scope of his or her employment is limited to answering the phone, greeting visitors, and signing for packages.

It gets more confusing when an employee creates software. In some cases, employee-created modifications of software owned by an employer have been deemed within the scope of

employment; in others, software created by an employee whose
duty it was to increase the standard of efficiency in a department has been deemed within the scope of employment, and
therefore a work made for hire.

If you are not an employee acting within the scope of your
employment (or these stretched definitions), the *only other
way* your work can fall into the work-for-hire classification is
if it meets *all* of three conditions set forth in the U.S. Copyright Law:

- *First,* the work must be specially ordered and commissioned. Thus a complete work submitted over the transom
  cannot qualify as a work for hire.
- *Second,* there must be an agreement in writing, signed by
  both parties, specifying that "the work shall be considered
  a work made for hire." The use of the word "shall" and
  dicta in the 1989 Supreme Court opinion on the subject
  suggest that such an agreement should antedate the creation of the work, but other case law suggests that it is
  possible to execute the written agreement at a later date
  if it confirms the previous understanding of the parties.
  Lawyers call this a *"nunc pro tunc"* agreement; that's
  Latin, meaning "now for then."
- *Third,* the work must fit into one of nine specific categories: compilations, translations, instructional texts,
  tests, answer materials for tests, atlases, supplementary
  works (defined in the law as works, such as forewords,
  illustrations, and indexes, prepared as adjuncts to a work
  by another author), contributions to collective works, and
  works prepared as part of a motion picture or other
  audiovisual work. If a freelancer's work does not fit into
  one of these categories, it cannot be a work for hire.

Remember, when your work falls into the classification of works made for hire, you are not considered its legal author— the commissioning party is! Not only is the term of copyright different, you have no copyright interest in the work. This holds true even though you may have received a byline on the work. Accept work-made-for-hire assignments only if you understand this and are willing to accept the consequences.

And bear in mind that when you sign a work-for-hire agreement, even if all three tests are not met, the court may interpret your signature as proof that you meant to assign all rights. Although an all-rights assignment can be terminated after thirty-five years, until and unless it *is*, the effect is the same as that of a work-made-for-hire assignment. See chapter 11 for more on this.

6.

What Good Is a
Copyright Anyway?

I've told you that a copyright is a "bundle of rights," but what's in that bundle? With certain limited exceptions, the owner of a copyright possesses—and can sell, license, or otherwise authorize the use of—five exclusive rights in a copyrighted work. These include the right to *reproduce* the work in copies and the right to *distribute* those copies to the public; it is these two rights that, when combined, constitute what we normally think of as "publishing" a work.

In general, the owner of the copyright also possesses the exclusive rights of public *performance* and *display*. Owning the performance right means that, with certain limited exceptions, a play cannot be performed without the copyright owner's consent. But it also means that an audio recording of a book (except for use by the hearing impaired) requires the same kind of authorization.

The display right as it applies to literary works does not so much protect an author from the display of his book in a bookstore as from having his poem carved into a wall without his permission. Public display of a work includes exhibiting or otherwise communicating a copy of it "by means of any device or process," whether members of the public receive it at the same place or in separate places, at the same time or at different times. If this sounds suspiciously like putting the work out on a computer bulletin board, you've hit on one of the rights the copyright law will protect.

The fifth exclusive right reserved to copyright owners is the right to prepare *derivative* works. These run the gamut from translating the work into a foreign language to translating it into another medium—dramatizing a novel, for example, or writing a book based on a television documentary. A sequel is a derivative work; so is every episode in a television series after the first, when such episodes use the same characters and take place in the same setting. A condensation is a derivative work, as is a revised second edition. Such works can be created only with the authorization of the copyright owner.

These five rights can be subdivided infinitely through the use of licenses and grants. For example, you can grant a magazine first North American serial rights—the right to publish your work in North America before any other magazine can do so—or you can license one-time rights, which means the magazine may publish the work once, with no guarantee that that will be the first time the piece appears. Granting first serial rights does not preclude the sale of book rights, and, unless you include film rights when you sign a book contract, selling book rights will not prevent you from selling the movie rights separately.

The sale of any or all of the five basic rights that make up a copyright and the sale of any part of any right can be restricted by time (performance rights for one year) or by geography (Icelandic serial rights) or by language (Urdu translation rights) or by medium (radio broadcast rights). When an exclusive right is licensed for a limited time, area, or medium, or when a nonexclusive right is granted, that right can be resold again and again. (You can, for example, sell one-time serial rights to any number of magazines. And once a license to create T-shirts or lunch boxes with your characters on them expires, you can grant that right to another manufacturer if you choose.)

It should be obvious by now that the sale of "all rights" can mean giving away a lot more than you bargained for. But the Copyright Law grants you not only the exclusive right to license these uses, it also grants you special remedies when someone exercises all or any one of these rights without your authority.

There are certain instances when unauthorized use may be legal. Making an archival copy of a computer program you have legitimately purchased, performing or displaying certain works in the course of a religious service, and nonprofit performances for the handicapped are among the uses that may not require the authorization of the copyright owner if certain conditions are met. Sometimes the exploitation of one or more of the five rights reserved to a copyright holder will qualify as a "fair use," a term I will discuss in more detail in chapter 8.

However, unless one of these exceptions applies, the copyright owner (or anyone who has received an *exclusive* license from the copyright owner) can bring suit for the unauthorized exploitation of any right he or she owns that is contained in the bundle of rights that comprises a copyright. Remedies include injunctions (court orders to discontinue the infringing act), the impounding and destruction of unauthorized copies of a copyrighted work, and monetary damages.

When a court orders an infringer to pay monetary damages to a copyright owner or licensee, the amount can include not only the actual damages (such as lost profits) suffered by the copyright owner but also any profits the infringer may have garnered through the use of the copyright material. (A recent case held an automobile company liable to pay an author a portion of the profits it earned during the time an infringing commercial ran on television!) In the alternative, statutory damages (which do not require proof of the copyright owner's actual loss or the infringer's actual gain) can be ordered. Statutory damages can range from $750 to $30,000, depending on what "the court considers just."

When a court decides that an infringement was willful it can increase an award of statutory damages to $150,000 (although the court can also reduce statutory damages to $200 when it finds that the infringer "was not aware and had no reason to believe that his or her acts constituted an infringement"). The court can also award "court costs and reasonable attorney's fees" when certain conditions have been met.

All of these rights and remedies can make a copyright a valuable commodity that is well worth protecting.

7.

Exploiting Your Copyrights

A copyright is a piece of property—what we lawyers call "intellectual property"—and like all property, its value is determined by the market that exists for it. A poem may have virtually no market; a play may never make it into production, or, when it does, may close on its opening night. A homespun article may garner $15 from your local weekly. Then again, a sizzling novel or kiss-and-tell exposé may earn a million-dollar advance.

Because the rights contained in a copyright can be divided and subdivided, it is possible to get a lot of mileage from a single copyright. One of the best examples I can cite is a Thanksgiving story that my mother wrote a number of years ago. She has sold and resold that story at least a dozen times to newspapers across the country—something she could do because she never signed a contract assigning the rights, and thus she still owns them all.

This would not have been the case before the 1976 copyright law revisions went into effect. Through December 31,

1977, it was presumed that when you submitted a story to a magazine or newspaper, you had assigned all rights for the first term of copyright in the absence of a contract to the contrary. If the publication had no further use for the piece, you could usually ask to have the rights reassigned to you, and you could then begin the sale process all over again. But if the publication would not or could not (if it was out of business, for example) revert the rights to you, you could not legally resell the piece until the first term of copyright was over.

Since January 1, 1978, the reverse has been true. In the absence of any express transfer of rights, it is assumed that the copyright in a work remains the possession of its creator. This is in keeping with the constitutional mandate "to secure . . . to Authors" the rights in their writings. Under the 1976 law, there is no involuntary transfer of copyright or any of the exclusive rights contained in a copyright (except under bankruptcy law, which I'll discuss later in chapter 12).

This means that you can't lose a copyright unless you sign it away—but a lot of writers do just that, usually out of eagerness to see their work in print. When you are offered a contract for your writing, read it carefully. Compare it, if you can, with contracts received by more experienced writers you may know. If you belong to a writers' group, for example, organize a contract bank so that members can compare the kinds of deals they are being offered by various publications. If you are eligible, join the Authors Guild; it provides members with a model contract and an explanation of key negotiating points. And read the "Rights" column in *Publishers Weekly*—but with a grain of salt. The deals that are reported there are likely to be unusual, or they wouldn't be deemed newsworthy.

When a contract involves a work that you think will have lasting value (as opposed to a story on yesterday's speech by the mayor), or when there is a considerable amount of money involved, run the contract by an experienced publishing lawyer. Or sign up with a savvy literary agent—if the contract is a legitimate one, you won't have any trouble getting an agent to take you on, because you've done half the work by getting a publisher to make an offer.

But note that I said a *legitimate* contract. The rule of thumb on this is publishers pay writers, not the other way around. Publishers who pay you are known as "risk publishers" because they risk *their* capital to publish *your* work. If someone has offered to publish your book for a fee, you are dealing with a vanity or subsidy press. Such publishers are seldom discriminating in what they publish; bookstores, distributors, and reviewers know this, and they often refuse to carry or review works published by vanity presses. Vanity presses hide behind a variety of smoke screens. Sometimes they offer what they call a "copublishing" deal, something that should be looked at long and hard—because if you wrote the book *and* you're paying for the actual cost of printing, why should they be receiving a share of the proceeds? Unless they are providing editorial services (at no cost to you), publicizing the book extensively, and providing access to a distributor, what exactly are they doing to merit the money?

This is not to say that what they're doing isn't legal—and, if you sign the contract, you will be bound by it. I've also seen another interesting variation in which the author was to pay nothing up front, but the publisher paid no royalties on the first 500 copies. My guess is that that publisher, who agreed to send out only twenty-five publicity copies (not nearly enough to get a book sold in fifty states!) and was not affiliated with any of the usual distribution companies, expected to make back the cost of printing by selling the author a large number of those first 500 copies at 50 percent off the cover price—*a price the publisher sets* and can jack up as high as it wants in order to boost its profits.

A publisher who charges to edit your book, or refers you to an affiliated editorial service, is also not the norm in the industry. While there *are* legitimate publishers who do not pay advances (indeed, that is often the case with textbook publishers and university presses), the author traditionally should not pay anything except the costs of permission to include the copyrighted works of others in the book, maps and the charts designed especially for the book, or outside indexing—and even payments for those things can be negotiated.

Of course, there are some instances in which paying to have your work published, or forgoing payments that would normally be due you, may be a reasonable course of action. If, for example, you want to publish something for which you know there will be only limited interest—a history of your family, for example—you probably will not be able to convince a commercial publisher to pay you for it. (*Roots* comes to mind as an exception to this rule, but that has already been done; you'd generally have to have an unusually interesting or notorious family to prompt a risk publisher to make an offer.)

If you think you can sell your book in conjunction with other work you do—presenting seminars, for example, or attending trade fairs—then it might pay for you to undertake the financial risk of publishing the work yourself in order to retain a higher percentage of the profit.

I firmly believe that the only other reason to pay to have your work published is if every legitimate publisher has turned you down, and you are nevertheless bound and determined to ignore this consensus in order to see your words in print. If you aren't spending the rent money or taking food off your table in order to fund your publishing venture, it is probably not much more of an exercise in futility than a trip to the gaming tables of Las Vegas or Atlantic City.

Should you choose this route, given the accessibility of desktop publishing, you can often save money by doing the work yourself—"self-publishing"—rather than signing an overpriced subsidy press contract. However, this requires that you shop around for quality services and a good price.

You can hire a freelance editor to check out your copy and you can do the layout and typesetting yourself with the help of a computer. If you have the spare cash, hire a book designer to help with layout. Then hire a printer or a local copy shop to do the printing and binding.

But producing the book is only half the battle. The main problems incurred by self-publishers are the same ones often incurred by authors whose books are published by vanity presses: obtaining distribution in the arcane world of book-selling and securing publicity and reviews. Since even books published by risk publishers are often ignored by reviewers and may receive limited publicity, this can prove a virtually insurmountable stumbling block for the amateur—the best argument I can think of for sticking with a professional publisher, who is invested in your book and has something to gain by promoting it.

As in any business dealings, when you work with publishers, written contracts should reflect the agreements you have come to. If they don't—or if they contain wording you don't understand—don't sign. Watch out for phrases like "all rights" and "work for hire." Remember, when you give away all rights or sign a work-for-hire contract, you no longer possess any of the five exclusive rights that the law grants to copyright owners.

This could mean you can't write a sequel to your novel, but that someone else of the publisher's choosing *can.*

Sign such agreements at your own risk, and only if you can modify them to a degree that makes *you* comfortable. For example, I once negotiated a license to reproduce and distribute, on a limited basis, a work-for-hire encyclopedia entry for the professor who wrote it, because she wanted to be allowed to distribute it to her students.

That noted, I'm tempted to add the old television caveat "Don't try this at home," because sometimes a publishing contract actually means something quite different from what it seems to say. I have seen book contracts that specifically provided for the registration of the copyright in the author's name but contained provisions that actually granted all rights, of every kind, to the publisher for the entire term of copyright. An author signing such a contract holds the copyright in name only, since he or she no longer possesses any of the rights that comprise the copyright.

This is not always an unconscionable circumstance. Where the publisher is better able to market the subsidiary rights than the author, and offers a fair split of the resulting sales, such an agreement can spell profit for both sides. However, it is important that anyone signing such a contract fully understand its terms and enter into the agreement knowledgeably and willingly.

Contrary to what most people believe, it is not necessary for a contract to be an unintelligible document full of obscure legal phrases. A simple letter that reflects the terms and conditions that the parties want will suffice. Sometimes a contract can be inferred from correspondence sent to confirm mutual discussions—and oral contracts *are* valid, especially if they can be proved by confirming correspondence or by the actions of the parties. However, the U.S. Copyright Law specifies that transfers of copyright—except "by operation of law," which normally means as a result of a court order—must be in writing and signed by the copyright owner.

Bear in mind, though, that once you sign any contract, it is almost always totally binding. It is always easier to turn down a contract than it is to get out of one. And *never* sign a contract with a point you don't want even though the other party has told you, "We can always change that later." Change terms you don't want *before* you sign the document.

Magazines often send assignment letters rather than full-fledged contracts. Even if they do not request that you sign one copy of the assignment letter and return it to them, if you follow the course of conduct set forth in the assignment— submitting an article of the required length on the specified subject by the stated deadline—it will generally be assumed that the terms of the assignment letter were acceptable to you unless there has been correspondence to the contrary.

But because magazines and other periodicals frequently fail to put anything about rights in writing, the U.S. Copyright Law deals with them—and other collective works—in a special section. This section states quite clearly that "copyright in each separate contribution to a collective work is distinct from copyright in the collective work as a whole, and vests initially in the author of the contribution." It goes on to say that where there is no express transfer of the copyright or of any rights under it, all that the collective work is presumed to have acquired is the right to publish the work "as part of that particular collective work, any revision of that collective work, and any later collective work in the same series."

While this technically means that the magazine could

republish your article in every issue without paying you anything more, this is unlikely to happen. And it clearly implies that the magazine has *not* acquired the right to reuse the work in any other publication, such as a book containing the "best of" the materials it has published, nor does it have the right to authorize others to publish the work. If it should do either, it is as guilty of infringing as is any other unauthorized user.

This issue came up in a case that went all the way to the Supreme Court. In 2001, in *New York Times Company, Inc., et al. versus Jonathan Tasini et al.*, the Court held that the *Times* did not have the right to sell articles it bought from freelancers to online services like Nexis, absent the written permission of the authors. The Court understood that once an article appears online, it loses its resale value. Alas, it was a Pyrrhic victory: now the *Times* usually requires such authorization from its contributors as part of the sale, as do many larger papers. You have to have a lot of clout (or some really valuable exclusive information) to negotiate an article sale to them without granting those rights.

8.

Thy Neighbor's Copyrights

When can you use materials created by others in your own works? The answer depends on the copyright status of those materials—whether they are in the public domain or are protected by copyright, and if they *are* protected, who has the authority to grant permissions concerning them.

When a work is in the public domain, it has no copyright protection. You can reproduce, distribute, perform, display, and adapt it at will. Generally, the only time you can rely on a work being in the public domain is when its first publication occurred more than ninety-five years ago, or when it was created more than 120 years ago, or when its authors (all of them) have been dead for more than seventy years.

It is possible for more recent works to have fallen into the public domain, but there is no hard-and-fast rule for determining when this has happened. For example, works published before 1978 without proper copyright notice normally fall into this unprotected category; however, if these works were foreign in origin, they may have been recaptured under the GATT and

NAFTA provisions discussed earlier. Pre-1964 works published with notice, if they were not renewed before their initial
twenty-eight-year term of copyright expired, also lapsed into
the public domain. And works first published between January
1, 1978, and March 1, 1989, either without notice or with
defective notice—if they did not fall into one of the exempt
categories or were not registered within five years of their initial publication—may also have lost their copyright protection.
In both instances, NAFTA and GATT exceptions apply.

Works of the U.S. government have no copyright protection,
but this is true only of the *federal* government, not state and
local governments. And even though works produced by the
federal government automatically fall into the public domain,
when protected works are included in any U.S. government
publication, their copyrights remain valid. The automatic
denial of copyright protection to works of the federal government does not apply to copyrighted works contained in government publications.

The copyright status of works should always be checked out
before you proceed with any use of them. Filings and registrations for works registered or renewed since January 1, 1978,
can be searched online through the copyright office website,
but information there is not conclusive as to copyright status.
If this information is not readily apparent, the Copyright Office
will investigate the copyright status of a work for $75 per hour
(this rate may be raised in the future to allow for inflation).
You must send payment for the first hour when you make your
request for information; they'll bill you if the matter involves
more time. Call (202) 707-6850 for further information.

Of course, since copyright registration is not mandatory, this
may not tell you much. You may need a copyright attorney to
help you ascertain whether a work is protected. And finding

out who owns the rights may require contacting the publisher, or the author, or conducting heirship research in the probate office of the county where the author last resided.

If a work is protected by copyright, you generally need the permission of the copyright owner before you can reproduce, quote from, or adapt it. Where some of the exclusive rights, such as film rights, have been transferred, you need the permission of the person who now holds them. You should never rely on an oral authorization; always obtain written proof when such permissions are granted.

Don't forget that pictorial, graphic, and sculptural works are also subject to copyright protection, so you must also obtain permission before reproducing them. Ownership of a painting does not confer ownership of the copyright in that painting, but for some reason this confuses many people who don't have any problem understanding copyrights in written works. Think of it this way: owning a copy of a book does not mean you own the copyright in that book, so why should owning a painting or a print mean you hold its copyright? With this in mind, it should be clear that you can't submit other people's maps, sketches, charts, and photos with your written works unless you have proper authorization to do so.

A picture in the public domain, such as the Gilbert Stuart portrait of George Washington, can, of course, be reproduced on the cover of your book, but if you *purchase*, rather than make, a slide of that picture, that slide may be protected by copyright. If, in photographing the original, the photographer did something (such as creating color separations) that required skill and added substantially to the original, the slide could be a derivative work, and the photographer would own those elements of it that were original.

The copyright in a photograph belongs to the photographer

because, under the 1976 law, copyrights normally belong to the creator of a work. If you want to reproduce a photo, you need the photographer's permission. This is true even if you have commissioned and paid for the photograph. Unless it qualifies as a work for hire—that is, if the photographer is your employee and taking photographs is part of his or her job, or if the three conditions for a freelance work for hire are met—you will need to obtain either a blanket permission for reuse or an assignment of rights before you can reproduce the work at will.

And since copyright law does not exist in a vacuum, even when you have permission, or when a work is in the public domain, other laws may prevent you from reproducing it—for example, when doing so would violate someone's right of privacy or publicity. Because an ordinary citizen has the right to keep his or her private life private and a celebrity has the right to choose if and when he or she will endorse certain products, such rights must be taken into consideration—even if you have the permission of the *copyright* owner—before you incorporate the works of others into your own materials.

And though a work may not be protected by copyright, if you reproduce it without proper attribution you may be guilty of plagiarism. Passing off another person's work as your own is bad form, to say the least; it can ruin your reputation if the truth comes out—and it *always* does—and it can cost you money if a lawsuit results. The remedy? Always credit your source—it's good manners, and it can help keep you clear of plagiarism accusations.

Sometimes you can use a work without permission even if it is protected by copyright, provided your use falls within the parameters of "fair use." The U.S. Copyright Law allows the reproduction, distribution, and adaptation of copyrighted material if the use is "for purposes such as criticism, comment, news reporting, teaching (including multiple copies for classroom use), scholarship, or research." This list is not exclusive; the words "such as" allow for its expansion, and parody, while not included in the list, has long been among the permitted uses.

But lest you think you have blanket permission to quote from or reproduce or otherwise exploit a copyrighted work if by some stretch of the imagination your work falls within one of these categories, you need to know that there are four factors that must be weighed before a use will qualify, and that most copyright scholars read the fair use section of the law as restrictive rather than permissive. This means that if you have any doubts, it is probably better to err on the side of caution and obtain permission whenever possible.

As the Supreme Court has noted, there is no "bright line" test of how much of a work you may use, or when, or under what circumstances. The fair use sections of the copyright law—which include limited special exemptions for librarians, educators, agricultural fairs, and religious services, among others—are intentionally imprecise, serving merely as general guidelines so that courts, users, and copyright owners can work out different definitions for different situations.

All of the four factors the law sets forth must be taken into consideration when determining whether a use is a *fair* use, though not all of them must be given equal weight. The four test factors as set forth in section 107 of Title 17 are:

1. *The purpose and character of the use, including whether it is of a commercial nature or is for nonprofit educational purposes.* Note that the law does not automatically bar all commercial uses (a parody, or a news commentary,

may well be commercial) nor does it automatically allow all nonprofit educational uses (course packs produced at cost may well be a violation of copyright, although different federal courts have recently divided on this point).

2. *The nature of the copyrighted work* itself—is it factual, such as a report of a health study that really can't be accurately paraphrased or summarized, or is it a rock song whose lyrics you want to weave through your article? In the former case, the greater public good may allow virtually verbatim copying. In the latter case, you would probably be infringing (although quoting most, if not all, of the lyric in an analytical article or scholarly critique, or even a parody, might well be permitted under the first factor).

3. *The amount and substantiality of the portion used in relation to the copyrighted work as a whole.* There is no set rule, such as a 500-word or eight-bar test, as many writers seem to think. Obviously, 500 words of a poem would often mean the entire poem; 500 words of an article could be half of it; but 500 words of a novel would be a relatively small amount. Note, however, that the law takes into account not only the amount but also the *substantiality* of the portion used. If a quote, however small, contains the substance of the original work, the use will probably not be considered "fair"; thus a relatively short excerpt from President Ford's memoirs, published without permission, was ruled an infringement by the Supreme Court, whereas some lower courts have since ruled that entire articles could be reproduced in order to discuss or critique them.

4. *The effect of the use upon the potential market for, or value of, the copyrighted work.* If the publication of a

portion of a work cuts into the sales potential of the whole work, costing the copyright owner money, the law may find infringement rather than fair use.

How much of a work *can* you use, then? The answer is a subjective one, and will vary with the circumstances surrounding a use. Even an expert can offer only his or her best guess. What I usually suggest is a kind of "golden rule" test—if *you* were the author of the original work, how would *you* feel about someone else using your work as you propose? If you are honest with yourself, your feelings can tell you a lot about how other copyright owners might feel.

Not only do you need permission to reprint all or part of someone else's copyrighted work (except in the case of a fair use), you also need permission to write your own story based on that work. When you create a derivative work, such as a play based on a novel or a new adventure story about someone else's characters, you generally hold the copyright in that derivative work to the extent that your creation is original. The new lines you have scripted, the new adventure you have cataloged, belong to you. However, because the copyright in the original work is not yours, you will need the copyright owner's permission before you can perform or publish the derivative work. (Technically, you need permission even to *prepare* a derivative work, but if it never sees the light of day during the term of copyright of the original, you're not likely to be sued for creating it.) And the copyright owner of the original work can demand the assignment of your copyright in it as a condition for granting you permission to create it.

And then there's parody. Sometimes the use of a character or setting is permitted when you are parodying the original work. Indeed, you're allowed to use as much of the original as you need to in order to conjure it up in the minds of your targeted audience. However, as always, each case will turn on its own special facts, and sometimes what *you* think is a parody will be found by a court to be an infringement.

The parody test tends to be even more subtle than the other fair use tests; the idea seems to be that you can satirize the work, but exploiting it to satirize society as a whole stretches the privilege to its breaking point. If your work competes with a legitimately licensed derivative work (thereby cutting into the profits of the copyright holder), you're probably infringing— but if your parody destroys the value of the original by holding it up to such ridicule that no one can ever think of it again with a straight face, the Supreme Court has suggested that that's quite lawful.

When your use does not fall within the fair use or parody exceptions, a two-part test will help determine if yours is an infringing use: (1) is your work *substantially similar* to the work you are alleged to have infringed, and (2) did you have *access* to the original work before or while you created yours?

Access may be presumed if there is only one person between you and the copyright holder—if the work was sent to you, and your secretary signed for it, it will be assumed that you saw it, that you had access. But if the work was sent to your secretary's brother, there is too much distance between you and the original. And a work submitted to the mailroom of a publisher will not be assumed to have reached either the editorial offices or another author whose work is later published by the company. However, if a work has been widely published, general public access may be presumed.

What constitutes substantial similarity? This is harder to call. One page out of a thousand could be used to prove infringement if that page is a verbatim copy of another, even unto the errors the original contained. More often substantial similarity will be premised on the volume of matching or parallel items—ten similar pages out of a hundred may not qualify as a substantial similarity, while ninety probably would.

The necessary similarity could also be established on the basis of a very similar general outline and a few specific instances of virtually identical text. A close paraphrase may also be deemed an infringement. However, no similarity is likely to be formed when both works have made use of the same *scènes à faire*.

One more note of caution: a revision is almost always a derivative work. If you don't own the copyright in a work, and have not obtained the right to prepare a derivative work based on it, you can't revise it—even if you wrote the original! If you assigned the copyright, or if the original work was created in the course of your employment (and is thus a work made for hire), you do not possess any rights in it. Under these circumstances, revising your work can be as much of an infringement as it would be if the original had been someone else's work.

In sum, the best way to protect yourself from running afoul of other people's copyrights is always to proceed with caution before using their materials, or to obtain permission, preferably in writing, to do so.

9.

Copyright Notice

You've probably seen copyright notices on published materials. People often assume that there is some secret to getting the right to put such a notice on your work.

There is—you must own the copyright. Since, as I have noted before, copyright exists from the moment an original work is fixed in a tangible medium of expression, you can put your notice on any of your work that is not work made for hire or for which you have not assigned the copyright, and you may do so as soon as the work is set down in any form.

A copyright notice is made up of three elements, all of which must be present for the notice to be valid:

- The *first* is the word "Copyright" or the abbreviation "Copr." or the symbol ©. The symbol must be the letter "C" in a circle, for visually perceptible copies; a ℗ is used on protected sound recordings.
- The *second* element is the year in which the work was first published. For an unpublished work such as a manuscript,

you may use the year in which that draft was completed, since copyright exists from the moment a work is created and exists in a partial work as well as a completed one. However, if your manuscript is subsequently published, the year of first publication should be substituted in the notice on the published work.

Sometimes a previously published work (such as an article or short story that has appeared in a magazine) is republished in an anthology. A single copyright notice on a magazine or anthology (the law terms these "collective works") will protect all the works contained in that collective work. When different parts of a collective work have different first publication dates, the year that the collective work as a whole is first published is sufficient for its copyright notice.

- The *third* element of proper notice is the name of the copyright holder. That usually means you, the author, unless you have made an assignment of your copyright (and remember that the commissioning party is the "author" when a work qualifies as a work made for hire). On a collective work, it is sufficient to use only the name of the person or company that owns the copyright in the collective work as a whole. Any abbreviation by which the name of the copyright owner can be recognized, and any generally known alternative designation of the owner, may be used in a notice.

Other phrases, such as "all rights reserved," are not necessary under U.S. law. Actually, for works published after March 1, 1989, even a copyright notice is not necessary. Inclusion of copyright notice on published works became optional for the preservation of copyright in a work after the United

States joined the Berne Convention. However, since the Berne Convention Implementation Act is not retroactive, the requirement that notice appear on works published before its effective date was not changed.

Even though copyright notice is no longer required, it is still a good idea to put it on all published works because including it affords extra protection for your copyright. When a published work bears a proper copyright notice, infringers cannot argue that they were misled by the lack of notice into assuming that the work was in the public domain. And as a practical matter, the notice may make it easier for someone seeking permission for the use of the work to find you.

The effect of omitting a copyright notice (or of including a defective one) depends on the law in effect when the work was first published. Works published before 1978, for example, were generally required to bear proper notice when published in order to preserve their copyrights.

Copyrights in works first published after January 1, 1978, but before March 1, 1989, were not automatically invalidated when a notice was omitted, incomplete, or defective. If the omission or defect occurred in no more than a relatively small number of the published copies, or if it was in violation of the express written requirement of the copyright owner that notice be published with the work, the protected status of the work was not affected. When these two exceptions did not hold, however, the work could be kept out of the public domain only if you registered it within five years of its publication and also made a "reasonable effort" to add the correct notice to all copies distributed after you discovered the omission or error.

What this has meant since January 1, 1978—even before the Berne changes went into effect—is that it has been a good idea to assume that all protectable works are indeed protected, because a work that bears no notice could be covered by one of the exceptions. And since no notice is required on works published after March 1, 1989, the assumption that all works are protected unless proven in the public domain should be standard operating procedure for anyone wanting to use copyrightable materials.

However, the best protection for your own works, no matter when they were first published, is to make sure the correct notice appears on them whenever they appear in print.

10.

Registration

People who don't realize that copyright exists in original works of authorship from the moment they are fixed in a tangible medium of expression often assume that there is some magic act that must be performed in order to "get a copyright." What comes closest to satisfying their expectations for that magic act is registration—the actual filing of a document in a government office, thus according the copyright official recognition.

But registration is generally an act that is *permitted* by the law, not *required* by it. The only occasion when current U.S. law requires that works be registered is before the commencement of a lawsuit for copyright infringement of any work whose "country of origin" is the United States (works originating in other Berne countries generally need not be registered before a suit is commenced).

Registration was previously required before a work first published prior to 1964 could be renewed. It was also a necessary step in the salvage of copyright in some works published without notice (or with insufficient or erroneous notice) before

March 1, 1989. If a new law work was registered before or within five years after the publication without notice occurred, the work did not fall into the public domain at the end of that five-year period—provided that in addition to registration, a "reasonable effort" was made to add notice to all copies distributed after the omission was discovered.

A work can be registered before it is published, but this is seldom necessary in the literary world; it is simply easier for a legitimate publisher to buy your piece than to commission someone else to duplicate your research and writing efforts. Individuals, however, may have no such constraints. And when you write lyrics or movie scripts, preregistration may prove helpful in the event a work that is substantially similar to yours appears on the market and you can prove that the producer or the person claiming to be the author had access to it. (For scripts, registration with the Writers Guild of America is also advisable; see chapter 17.) Generally, however, registering your writing before submitting it is not necessary and, indeed, is probably too expensive for the average writer.

One way to get around the expense is to assemble all of your unpublished works written in a specific period of time— say a year—into a single work, labeling it something like "The 1988 Unpublished Works of _____." This would enable you to register it for a single fee. Unfortunately, if someone infringed only one of the works contained in the collection— even if that work was reprinted in its entirety—the question of whether it was a substantial portion of the whole collection could be raised as a defense. And the titles of the individual works contained in the collection will not appear in the Copyright Office records, although the entire collection will remain archived should proof of the work's inclusion be disputed.

Prepublication registration is the main exception to the rule that a work can be registered only once; a work registered before publication can be registered after it is published. However, once a *published* work is registered, only if it is *substantially* altered is another registration possible. To register the new version, you must explain on the application form how it differs from the original.

How do you register a work? First you will need to obtain the proper forms from the Copyright Office or its website (see chapter 23). Line-by-line instructions for filing copyright forms come with them, and since the information *you* put on the copyright form is the information you will have to live with in the event your copyright is ever litigated, it is a good idea to be extra careful in filling out the application. If you are uncertain of how to proceed after reading the instructions, you can call the Copyright Office's Public Information Office—(202) 707-3000—for assistance. If after that you're still not sure how to proceed, or if your problem appears to be more complex, consult a copyright lawyer; the Public Information Office can give assistance, but they can't give legal advice.

Which form you file depends on the kind of work you are registering. For most written works, whether published or unpublished, you should use Form TX or Short Form TX. If you run short of space on Form TX, the additional information goes on a Continuation Sheet (Form _____/CON), which should be submitted with Form TX. Plays and scripts should generally be registered using Form PA.

When registering unpublished works, submit only one copy of the work; for published works, two copies of the "best edition" of the work (Copyright Office Circular 7b discusses just what qualifies as the "best edition") are generally required. However, for contributions to collective works—a short story included in an anthology or an article published in a magazine, for example—only one copy is required. Previously, a *complete* copy of the best edition of the collective work in which your work appeared was required, and you were advised not to clip your article out of the magazine, but to submit the entire issue. Recently, this rule has been amended to allow for photocopies or tear sheets. The details can be found on the Copyright Office website (www.copyright.gov).

Include your check or money order for the filing fee, made payable to "Register of Copyrights." If you submit a check rather than a money order, your canceled check will bear a number that can be useful should you need to trace the registration (although the Copyright Office won't initiate a trace unless more than sixteen weeks have elapsed since the application was submitted).

The form, the fee, and the copy or copies should all be submitted *in the same package*. If you send your registration by certified or registered mail, with a return receipt request, you will have proof of delivery and a record of the date the Copyright Office received your materials. This is a useful reference until the registration document is returned, because copyright registrations are generally effective as of the day the Copyright Office receives them.

Because the Copyright Office is part of the Library of Congress and is located on Capitol Hill, "all U.S. Postal Service and Private carrier mail is being screened off-site" since 2001. This may add three to five days to the delivery time.

If your works appear regularly in periodicals, you may want to take advantage of a special money-saving provision in the U.S. Copyright Law that allows you to register all your works that have been published in periodicals within any twelve-month period (it needn't be a calendar year) for a single registration fee. The basic copyright registration fee at this writing is $30.

You do this by filing adjunct Form GRCP together with Form TX or Form PA, whichever applies to your work. You must also submit one complete copy of the periodical in which your work appeared (for newspapers, a complete copy of the section in which the work appeared is sufficient). You were previously advised not to clip your work from the periodical. Now alternatives are available; check the Copyright Office website or call the Public Information Office for details.

Works registered using Form GRCP must all be the work of a single author, must all have the same copyright claimant, and cannot be works made for hire. For works published before March 1, 1989, each work as first published had to have borne its own copyright notice, separate from that of the periodical in which it appeared—and the same copyright owner had to have been named in each of those separate notices; for works published since the effective date of the Berne amendments to the U.S. Copyright Law, this separate notice is no longer required.

If you find you have made an error on a filing, or have left something off, you can file Form CA to correct or amplify a previous registration. All copyright forms can be ordered from the Copyright Office in Washington, D.C., and you may reproduce the forms or download them from the Copyright Office website, so long as the copies are of good quality, on white paper, 8½ inches by 11 inches in size, *and reproduced in two-sided copies, head-to-head*—that is, with the top of the back at the same end as the top of the front.

But if registration is optional, why register at all?

There are a number of good reasons. For example, if you

FORM TX

For a Nondramatic Literary Work
UNITED STATES COPYRIGHT OFFICE

REGISTRATION NUMBER

_____

TX _____ TXU _____

EFFECTIVE DATE OF REGISTRATION

_____

Month _____ Day _____ Year

DO NOT WRITE ABOVE THIS LINE. IF YOU NEED MORE SPACE, USE A SEPARATE CONTINUATION SHEET.

1

TITLE OF THIS WORK ▼

PREVIOUS OR ALTERNATIVE TITLES ▼

PUBLICATION AS A CONTRIBUTION If this work was published as a contribution to a periodical, serial, or collection, give information about the collective work in which the contribution appeared. **Title of Collective Work ▼**

If published in a periodical or serial give: Volume ▼   Number ▼   Issue Date ▼   On Pages ▼

2

a

NAME OF AUTHOR ▼

DATES OF BIRTH AND DEATH
Year Born ▼   Year Died ▼

Was this contribution to the work a "work made for hire"?
☐ Yes
☐ No

AUTHOR'S NATIONALITY OR DOMICILE
Name of Country
OR { Citizen of ▶ _____
Domiciled in ▶ _____

WAS THIS AUTHOR'S CONTRIBUTION TO THE WORK
Anonymous? ☐ Yes ☐ No
Pseudonymous? ☐ Yes ☐ No
If the answer to either of these questions is "Yes," see detailed instructions.

NATURE OF AUTHORSHIP Briefly describe nature of material created by this author in which copyright is claimed. ▼

NOTE

Under the law, the "author" of a "work made for hire" is generally the employer, not the employee (see instructions). For any part of this work that was "made for hire" check "Yes" in the space provided, give the employer (or other person for whom the work was prepared) as "Author" of that part, and leave the space for dates of birth and death blank.

b

NAME OF AUTHOR ▼

DATES OF BIRTH AND DEATH
Year Born ▼   Year Died ▼

Was this contribution to the work a "work made for hire"?
☐ Yes
☐ No

AUTHOR'S NATIONALITY OR DOMICILE
Name of Country
OR { Citizen of ▶ _____
Domiciled in ▶ _____

WAS THIS AUTHOR'S CONTRIBUTION TO THE WORK
Anonymous? ☐ Yes ☐ No
Pseudonymous? ☐ Yes ☐ No
If the answer to either of these questions is "Yes," see detailed instructions.

NATURE OF AUTHORSHIP Briefly describe nature of material created by this author in which copyright is claimed. ▼

c

NAME OF AUTHOR ▼

DATES OF BIRTH AND DEATH
Year Born ▼   Year Died ▼

Was this contribution to the work a "work made for hire"?
☐ Yes
☐ No

AUTHOR'S NATIONALITY OR DOMICILE
Name of Country
OR { Citizen of ▶ _____
Domiciled in ▶ _____

WAS THIS AUTHOR'S CONTRIBUTION TO THE WORK
Anonymous? ☐ Yes ☐ No
Pseudonymous? ☐ Yes ☐ No
If the answer to either of these questions is "Yes," see detailed instructions.

NATURE OF AUTHORSHIP Briefly describe nature of material created by this author in which copyright is claimed. ▼

3

a

YEAR IN WHICH CREATION OF THIS WORK WAS COMPLETED This information must be given in all cases. ◀ Year

b

DATE AND NATION OF FIRST PUBLICATION OF THIS PARTICULAR WORK
Complete this information ONLY if this work has been published.
Month ▶ _____ Day ▶ _____ Year ▶ _____ ◀ Nation

4

See instructions before completing this space.

COPYRIGHT CLAIMANT(S) Name and address must be given even if the claimant is the same as the author given in space 2. ▼

TRANSFER If the claimant(s) named here in space 4 is (are) different from the author(s) named in space 2, give a brief statement of how the claimant(s) obtained ownership of the copyright. ▼

DO NOT WRITE HERE / OFFICE USE ONLY

APPLICATION RECEIVED

ONE DEPOSIT RECEIVED

TWO DEPOSITS RECEIVED

FUNDS RECEIVED

MORE ON BACK ▶ • Complete all applicable spaces (numbers 5-9) on the reverse side of this page.
• See detailed instructions.   • Sign the form at line 8.

DO NOT WRITE HERE

Page 1 of _____ pages

Full-size copies of Form TX are available from the Copyright Office or its website; use this form or the Short Form TX when registering most written materials, whether published or unpublished, other than scripts and entire periodicals.

PREVIOUS REGISTRATION Has registration for this work, or for an earlier version of this work, already been made in the Copyright Office?

☐ Yes ☐ No If your answer is "Yes," why is another registration being sought? (Check appropriate box.) ▼

a. ☐ This is the first published edition of a work previously registered in unpublished form.

b. ☐ This is the first application submitted by this author as copyright claimant.

c. ☐ This is a changed version of the work, as shown by space 6 on this application.

If your answer is "Yes," give: **Previous Registration Number** ▶   **Year of Registration** ▶

5

DERIVATIVE WORK OR COMPILATION

Preexisting Material Identify any preexisting work or works that this work is based on or incorporates. ▼

Material Added to This Work Give a brief, general statement of the material that has been added to this work and in which copyright is claimed. ▼

a

b

6

See instructions before completing this space.

DEPOSIT ACCOUNT If the registration fee is to be charged to a Deposit Account established in the Copyright Office, give name and number of Account.

Name ▼   **Account Number** ▼

a

7

CORRESPONDENCE Give name and address to which correspondence about this application should be sent.   Name / Address / Apt / City / State / ZIP ▼

b

Area code and daytime telephone number ▶   Fax number ▶

Email ▶

CERTIFICATION* I, the undersigned, hereby certify that I am the

Check only one ▶

☐ author

☐ other copyright claimant

☐ owner of exclusive right(s)

☐ authorized agent of _____

of the work identified in this application and that the statements made by me in this application are correct to the best of my knowledge.

Name of author or other copyright claimant, or owner of exclusive right(s) ▲

8

Typed or printed name and date ▼ If this application gives a date of publication in space 3, do not sign and submit it before that date.

_____ Date ▶ _____

Handwritten signature (X) ▼

X _____

9

Certificate will be mailed in window envelope to this address:

Name ▼

Number/Street/Apt ▼

City/State/ZIP ▼

prevail in court against an infringer, you can recover those statutory damages I mentioned in chapter 6 *and reimbursement of your attorney's fees* only if registration has been made before the infringement commences. If you register after the infringement begins, not only will you have to pay your own attorney's fees, but any monetary award you receive will be limited to your actual losses and the infringer's profits—both of which can be very difficult to prove.

Note, however, that the law grants a three-month grace period after first publication of a work: you can still recover statutory damages and attorney's fees for an infringement that occurs after your work has been published but before registration if you register within that grace period. But be forewarned when using Form GRCP to register all of your works published within a twelve-month period that if you wait for the end of that period, works published earlier in the year may have exceeded the three-month grace period. If they are infringed prior to the group registration, you will forfeit the right to statutory damages and attorney's fees, just as you would have if you'd used Form TX.

When you register within five years of first publication, your claim of copyright ownership and any other facts regarding the copyright that are stated on the registration document will be considered prima facie evidence—evidence that the court will accept as true unless the opposing party can present conclusive evidence to the contrary. This is a good reason to be extremely careful in filling out the registration forms; so is the fact that "[a]ny person who knowingly makes a false representation of a material fact in the application for copyright registration" can be fined up to $2,500.

Also, as I mentioned earlier, for works whose country of origin is the United States (essentially, any work first published in the United States, or any work that either is unpublished or is first published in a non-Berne country if all of its authors are citizens of, or habitually reside in, the United States), registration *must* be made before an infringement suit can be filed. Since injunctions, impounding, and destruction of infringing works are among the remedies for copyright infringement (in addition to monetary damages), the more quickly you can bring a suit, the more quickly you can get infringing goods off the market. Unfortunately, it can take a considerable amount of time to get the registration documents back from the Copyright Office (I've often experienced a wait of over six months), so if you think there is any likelihood that your work will be infringed, early registration is one way to speed things up.

An expeditious filing procedure is available, but only if circumstances, such as an impending lawsuit, warrant it—and it is expensive. You must submit two copies of the best edition of the work, together with the appropriate form, your filing fee, and an additional payment of $580: Payment must be by certified check, cashier's check; or money order made payable to the Register of Copyrights. Special handling requests should include the Copyright Office form entitled "Request for Special Handling" if you have it; if you do not, you must include a cover letter requesting special handling and explaining why you need it, and how soon. These applications go to a *special address*:

> Special Handling
> Copyright Receiving and Processing
> Box 71380
> Washington, D.C. 20024-1380

Do not put the words "Copyright Office" on the envelope, or it will get buried in the avalanche of mail that the Copyright Office receives every day and will not receive the special handling you need. For more information, order Copyright Circular 10 or get it online at the website (www.copyright.gov/circs/circ10.pdf).

If you are publishing your work yourself, there is another good reason for registering it: the copies submitted with a registration application satisfy the deposit requirement. Two copies of all works published in the United States—except for certain categories of work exempt by law or by special regulation (for example, limited numbered editions)—must be deposited with the Library of Congress within three months of their first publication. If you fail to make a deposit, the Register of Copyrights can demand, in writing, that you do so. The collection of the Library of Congress is built on these deposits, so this requirement is taken seriously. Failure to comply with a demand for a deposit can result in a fine of $250 per work—and an additional fine of $2,500 for willfully or repeatedly failing to comply.

Incidentally, if you are publishing a newsletter or other periodical, you can group register a number of issues to keep the registration costs down. Which form you use—Form SE, Short Form SE, or Form SE/Group—depends, among other things, on the copyright ownership of contributions and the frequency of publication. Send for Copyright Office Circulars 62 and 62a for more details.

Obviously, if you are a publisher who hasn't been making the required deposits, you should at least make sure you have enough archival copies on hand to do so if requested. Check with the Copyright Office or with a copyright lawyer to determine if your publications are exempt. If they are not, the required deposits should be made promptly.

If you deposit the required copies and later decide to register the work you've deposited, you will have to submit two additional copies with your registration application and fee. However, when you register a work, the copies submitted with the registration application satisfy the deposit requirement and no additional deposit need be made.

If you cannot locate two copies of the best edition of your work (or even one copy of the best edition of a collective work in which your work appeared)—or if sending them in might pose a financial hardship—it is sometimes possible to obtain permission to substitute other materials with your registration application. To do this, you must petition the Copyright Office, in writing, for "special relief." Your request should explain why you cannot send the required materials and should indicate what you wish to submit instead. Bear in mind, however, that such requests are not granted without good reason, so you should not count on obtaining special relief when you lack the required deposit copies.

One last reason for registering your work: although registration can be made anytime during the period that a work is covered by copyright, the Copyright Office can increase fees at intervals as costs warrant. Registering as soon as possible can save you the higher fee that may be in effect at a later date.

The Copyright Office now has made new Short Forms TX and PA available. A *living author* (not a corporation) may use the Short Forms if he or she is the sole author and sole copyright owner of the work being registered. And "[t]he work must be completely new in the sense that it does not contain substantial material that has been previously published or registered or that is in the public domain."

Works made for hire may not be registered using the Short Forms, nor are these forms "appropriate for an anonymous author who does not wish to reveal his or her identity." Check the instructions carefully to determine which form is right for you.

11.

Renewal, Restoration, and Termination

U.S. copyright protection in works first published *after* January 1, 1978, currently extends seventy years after the death of the author (or the last surviving joint author). For works first published *before* January 1, 1978—even if first publication occurred as late as December 31, 1977—it's another story.

Copyright duration now depends on a number of things—not only the age of the work, but also whether the work is a U.S. work or a foreign one still subject to protection in its source country, whether there was compliance with all of the formalities (such as copyright notice or American manufacture) the U.S. law required at the time of its publication, and whether the work was renewed in the twenty-eighth year after its publication.

You really do need a scorecard to tell the players when calculating the duration of a work published as late as February 28, 1989. First of all, there are those formalities: if the work was published before January 1, 1978, without proper copyright notice, or before July 1, 1986, in violation of the now defunct manufacturing clause (which, in essence, required that printing be done in the United States or Canada), it fell into the public domain. If the notice was erroneous or was omitted from copies published between January 1, 1978, and March 1, 1989, it was possible to effect a cure, but if the appropriate steps were not taken (as discussed in chapter 9), the work lost its copyright protection.

With the passage of the Copyright Renewal Act of 1992, works were divided not only by those in compliance and those that were not, but also by whether they required formal renewal (if first published before January 1, 1964) or were automatically entitled to seventy-five-year protection (if first published after that date but before the new law went into effect). Those works still protected by copyright in 1998 had twenty more years added to their renewal term; those that entered the public domain in 1997 did not.

With the passage of the Uruguay Round Agreements Act (by which the United States ratified the General Agreement on Tariffs and Trade, or GATT, and joined the World Trade Organization, or WTO) in 1994—and, to a lesser degree, with the passage of the North American Free Trade Agreement (NAFTA) the year before, a new division between copyright owners was created. Now there are U.S. works and works for which the source country is "a nation other than the United States."

To a certain extent, this foreign-versus-American division already existed as a result of U.S. adherence to the Berne Convention as of March 1, 1989. After that date, although U.S. copyright holders were required to register their copyrights before bringing suit for copyright infringement in American courts, copyright holders from other Berne countries were not. Since the ratification of NAFTA and the GATT, however, it has been possible for foreign copyright holders to recapture copyrights that had been forfeited for failure to comply with American formalities such as the notice or renewal requirements or the manufacturing clause.

To qualify for copyright restoration, a work must have been less than seventy-five (now ninety-five) years old, must still have been copyrighted in the source country, must have lost its U.S. copyright for failure to comply with American formalities, and the source country must be a member of the World Trade Organization. Restoration is automatic when a country joins the WTO, but enforcement of the copyright against those who—relying on its previous public domain status—had already exploited it, requires the service of a Notice of Intent to Enforce a Restored Copyright on the reliance party at any time or the filing of such a notice with the U.S. Copyright Office within two years of restoration.

So here's that scorecard for the most common duration problems (all terms expire December 31):

- If a work was first published before January 1, 1978, without copyright notice, it lapsed into the public domain, where it remains, unless it is a foreign work eligible for copyright recapture, in which case its copyright endures for ninety-five years (unless its seventy-five-year term of copyright expired before January 1, 1998).
- If a work was first published between January 1, 1978, and March 1, 1989, without notice, the omission could be cured. If it was, the copyright endures for the life of the author plus seventy years, unless it was anonymous, pseudonymous, or a work made for hire, in which case its term ends ninety-five years after its first publication, or 120 years after its creation, whichever comes first. If it was

not cured, and it is a U.S. work, it has fallen into the public domain and remains there, but if it is a foreign work, its copyright is eligible for restoration.

• If the work was first published before January 1, 1964, its copyright endured for twenty-eight years, and unless it was renewed in the twenty-eighth year, it fell into the public domain at the end of that year; foreign works that fell into the public domain for failure to renew can, however, be reinstated, although U.S. works cannot. If the work was renewed before the end of the twenty-eighth year after its first publication, its renewal term was forty-seven years if the forty-seven years ran out during 1997, but sixty-seven years if it was still under copyright in 1998. In that case, its copyright—whether foreign or domestic—expires at the end of the ninety-fifth year.

• If the work was first published between January 1, 1964, and December 31, 1977, its copyright endures for ninety-five years. This ninety-five-year period is divided into two terms, the first of twenty-eight years and the second of sixty-seven; and if the copyright is renewed in the twenty-eighth year, its ownership and control can be affected.

• If the work was unpublished as of January 1, 1978, its term is the life of the author plus seventy years, but in no case did it expire before the end of 2002—and if it was published before that date, it endures until the end of 2047, even if the author has been dead for centuries.

And what about those renewals? Why make them if the term is now automatically ninety-five years? Formal renewal made in the twenty-eighth year can be advantageous for several reasons. One is that if the author is still alive in the twenty-eighth year, and has made a grant or assignment of rights, the grantee can cement that grant by renewal. Although an author may be bound by contract to grant exploitation rights for the renewal term, a deceased author's heirs cannot be bound except by their own agreement—so if the author dies before the renewal is made, the renewal right will belong to the author's spouse and children and the grant will no longer be valid. And their renewal in the twenty-eighth year cuts off the right to continued exploitation of any derivative works that were licensed by the author during the first term. This can mean money for an author's heirs, for if a movie has been made from a novel, the moviemaker cannot continue to show it without renegotiating for the rights. If heirs fail to make a formal renewal during the twenty-eighth year, the film can continue to be exploited, although no remakes will be allowed.

You renew by filing Form RE, accompanied by the appropriate fee; no copies need be submitted with the renewal application. However, if you did not register the work prior to renewal, the Register of Copyrights may request the information that could have been included with your registration, so it may be simpler to register at the time you renew.

A group of works can be renewed with a single application if all were written by the same author, were first published in periodicals and were copyrighted under the laws then in effect (this usually meant publication *with notice*), were published during the same *calendar* year, and are being claimed by the same renewal claimant on the same basis (for example, as author). Each work must be separately identified in the renewal application, along with the periodical in which it appeared and the date of its first publication.

Who renews the copyright? If the author is living at the time the renewal application is filed, he or she may claim the renewal unless the work was made for hire, or unless he or she previously assigned the renewal right. If the author dies before the renewal application is filed, his or her surviving spouse or children, or both, may renew the registration, even if the author previously assigned the renewal right to someone else.

If the author leaves no surviving spouse or children, but does leave a will, the executor or executors named in the will may claim the renewal. In the absence of a surviving spouse or child *and* of a will, the author's next of kin (as designated under the laws of the state where the author resided) may claim the renewal right.

Inheriting a renewal right is not the same thing as inheriting a copyright. The renewal right exists only in works first published before January 1, 1978. The exercise of the renewal right could conceivably overturn the bequest of an old-law work made in an author's will, if the beneficiary named in the will is not in line to inherit the renewal right. As noted earlier, if a timely renewal application is made, previous grants and licenses can be overturned.

There is another right by which the law allows an author or his or her heirs to override previous grants of copyright (except those made by will). This is the *termination right.* Termination rights are inalienable—they cannot be assigned to anyone else. But they also require action on the part of the persons entitled to them. If a termination right is not exercised at the proper time, it lapses and cannot be recovered. The copyright continues to exist, but it cannot be reacquired, without consent, from the person or corporation to whom it was assigned.

The rules for exercising a termination right are complex, and those seeking to exercise them may require legal assistance to do so properly. Among the complicating factors: different grantors have different termination rights (depending on when the grant was made and who made it, i.e., the author or someone other than the author who owned the rights), and termination rights, when they exist, may or may not be inheritable.

For example, if the grant of a copyright or the rights contained in it was made *before* January 1, 1978, the person granting the rights—whether or not the grantor was the author—may terminate it after *fifty-six years*. This is because, under the 1909 law, copyright renewal terms lasted twenty-eight years, not forty-seven or sixty-seven, so the total term of copyright was fifty-six years; when the 1976 law was passed, it was thought unfair to include the extra nineteen (now thirty-nine) years in the grant without giving the grantor a chance to get them back.

Where assignments of rights are made *starting* January 1, 1978, whether in old- or new-law works, terminations may be effected *thirty-five* years after the grant is made on two- to ten-year prior written notice. A nonauthor making an assignment of rights after January 1, 1978, does not have the right to terminate that assignment, although a deceased author's heirs may terminate grants *made by the author*.

The law prescribes a hierarchy of people who may exercise the termination right. For old-law works, *a grant made by someone other than the author* can be terminated (after fifty-six years) only by "the surviving person or persons who executed it." The grantor's heirs do not inherit the right to terminate the grant.

In both old- and new-law works, *where the grant was made by the author*, the right of termination belongs first to the author, if living, then to his or her surviving spouse (to be shared, in proportions designated by the law, with surviving children or grandchildren, if any). If there is no surviving spouse, the right is shared by the author's surviving children and grandchildren.

All shares belonging to children and grandchildren are "per stirpes"—meaning essentially that children share equally, and children of any deceased child share that child's interest equally. In cases where a termination right is shared, those holding the majority interest prevail when there's a dispute.

Terminations are *not* automatic. The right must be exercised within a five-year term beginning at the end of the pretermination period, whether thirty-five or fifty-six years, on two- to ten-year advance notice. The procedure for termination is outlined in sections 203 and 304 of the U.S. Copyright Law. If a termination right is not exercised within the specified period, it lapses and cannot be recaptured; the recipient of the original grant continues to hold the rights unless he or she assigns them, until the end of the term of copyright.

Because of the lengthy time periods involved before termination or renewal rights can be exercised, it can be all too easy for an author or his heirs to miss a deadline for renewing a copyright or terminating an assignment of rights. For this reason, I generally advise authors to *maintain a list* of any grants or assignments they make, the date the grants were made, and the person or corporation to whom the rights were granted; this list, together with copies of any contracts the author may have signed for major works, should be kept where the author (or his heirs) can easily locate them. It might also be a good idea to include a copy of sections 203 and 304 of the copyright law with this list, so that heirs happening upon it will understand the value of the list—if not the wording, which is *very* complex, of the law.

12.

Bankruptcy and Wills

The initial transfer of an individual author's copyright or any of the rights contained in it can occur only when the author makes a voluntary assignment of those rights, except when the author files for bankruptcy. Bankruptcy, like copyright, is authorized under Article I, clause 8 of the Constitution, which gives Congress the power to establish "uniform laws on the subject of bankruptcies throughout the United States."

Bankruptcy is a means of wiping the slate clean of your debts and starting over. When you file for bankruptcy, the court sets aside certain minimal assets you may keep, then liquidates the rest of your assets (termed the "estate"), assigning the proceeds to your creditors, generally in proportion to how much you owe them.

Because copyrights are property, they are subject to seizure and sale under bankruptcy law. If they are of negligible value, the Trustee in Bankruptcy who has been assigned to liquidate your estate may choose to abandon them, in which case you continue to own them. However, if any of your copyrights appear to have some value, the trustee may offer them for sale either privately (in which case you may have the opportunity to purchase them yourself) or at public auction, with the proceeds going to your creditors. The purchaser would have the right to exploit the copyrights or any other rights purchased at such a sale.

The only other way that copyrights are subject to what amounts to involuntary transfer is when they pass to your heirs under intestate succession laws—the laws applying to people who die without a valid will. When you make a will, you choose who will receive your property—including your copyrights—after your death. When you die without a will, state law determines who will receive your assets and possessions. In some states, depending on how distant a relative your "next of kin" is, if you leave no will, your property may be forfeited to the state.

Intestate succession laws generally mandate that your property will pass to your next of kin, although the definition of "next of kin" may vary, for inheritance purposes, from state to state. In some states, your surviving spouse gets everything; in other states, your spouse and children must share according to a formula. If you leave no surviving spouse or children, your estate may go to your parents or, if they are no longer living, to your brothers and sisters in equal shares. When that is the case, the children of any deceased sibling will generally receive his or her share.

When you make a will, you can divide your rights and copyrights the way you can any property. You might specify that the copyright in your book of poetry go to your cousin Mary and the movie rights in your novel go to your brother Joe. Generally, this cuts out all other contenders. Even where there are no specific bequests of this kind, writers should always make sure to inform the attorneys drafting their wills that for them the term "property" includes *intellectual* property.

This can make a difference in the tax aspects of an estate plan, and it might also be important where you have heirs who may not understand the best ways to exploit the rights in literary works. If you have valuable literary properties—such as a best-selling novel or a steadily selling how-to book—and if your heirs are minors or, perhaps, have no sense of the publishing business, you might want to put your copyrights in trust. The trust can be administered by someone who knows the literary world—perhaps your agent or a good friend who is familiar with the field—with the proceeds going to the heirs you designate as trust beneficiaries.

And, as I mentioned previously, it is also a good idea to leave a list of any assignments of rights you may have made, together with copies of the contracts you have signed concerning your writing, someplace where your heirs can find them easily. You might also want to include a copy of this book, some similar publication, or Title 17 (the copyright law), so your heirs will know how to make use of the information you've provided them.

One further cautionary note for those who live in community property states or who may be contemplating either marriage or divorce: copyrights are property and if acquired during a marriage may be *community* property. Make sure the lawyer drafting your prenuptial agreement or handling your divorce knows you own them.

13.

Contracts

All of the rights in a written work do not necessarily involve copyright. For example, getting paid for your work may involve contract law or—in a worst-case scenario—bankruptcy law.

The copyright law requires that a transfer of copyright ownership (other than transfers made "by operation of law," such as bankruptcy proceedings) must be made *in writing*, and that writing must be signed by the owner of the copyright, or by the owner's duly authorized agent. By "agent," the law does not necessarily mean a literary agent, and, indeed, most authors do not authorize their literary agents to sign their contracts for them, only to negotiate them.

But any time you authorize someone to act on your behalf— to pick up your cleaning at the dry cleaner or to sign for a package that is being delivered, for example—you are authorizing them to act as your agent. Generally, such authorizations are limited, but possession of a general power of attorney will allow someone to deal with your property as though it were their own—and that includes the power to assign copyrights.

It follows that you should restrict powers of attorney when you issue them, and that you should carefully watch the language in any contract with your agent. (Of course, you do *have* a contract with your agent, don't you?) In the interest of preserving a good working relationship, it is also a good idea to have written contracts between writers collaborating on a work, and between writer and subject, especially if an exclusive relationship is contemplated.

Such contracts should stipulate not only when the relationship commences and what works it involves, but also how it can be terminated and what rights and responsibilities will survive its termination. A contract should delineate each party's rights, responsibilities, and compensation, and should also outline the remedies available in case the other party fails to live up to his or her obligations.

Contracts need not be *written* to be valid. An oral contract is valid—the difficulty is in proving its terms if a disagreement develops between the parties. For this reason, it is always a good idea to reduce a contract to writing.

Where books are concerned, there is almost always a contract—and it is almost always negotiable, for, as I indicated in chapter 7, a written contract is nothing more than a document on which the agreement of two or more parties has been set down. The basic rule here is, if you don't agree with the terms, don't sign the contract, for by signing it, you are indicating your approval and acceptance of them.

Magazines will sometimes send you contracts; more often, they will send you an assignment letter telling you what they want, when they want it, and how much they will pay. If you turn in an article of the specified length, on the specified topic, by the specified date, you will have fulfilled your part of the contract, and their obligation will be to pay you for the material you submitted as specified in the assignment letter. In other words, the letter and your resulting actions define the contract.

A contract is normally made up of an offer, the acceptance of that offer, and the definition of the compensation involved. When you propose a work to a publisher, you have made an offer, and a letter accepting your work for publication for a specific sum constitutes a counteroffer. If you accept the terms offered by the publisher, a contract will exist.

When you submit a completed piece to a magazine or newspaper, it is generally assumed that you are willing to accept that publication's customary payment terms. Often, your first indication that the piece has been published will be the arrival of a check—and perhaps a contributor's copy—in the mail. As noted in chapter 7, there is a special provision in the U.S. Copyright Law for stories, articles, sketches, cartoons, or photographs that are published as part of a collective work where there is no written agreement concerning the transfer of rights. The collective work acquires the right to publish your piece only "as part of that particular collective work, any revision of that collective work, and any later collective work in the same series."

While copyright law deals with the use of your work, it is silent as to how or when you should be compensated, when the work will be published, and whether you will receive a copy. These things are defined by custom or by contract or in an assignment letter.

If you don't receive a contract or an assignment letter from someone who wants to publish your work, or if what you do receive doesn't contain a provision you feel is important—for example, how much you will be paid, and *when*—you can call or write to find out the publication's policy in such matters; once you come to an agreement, ask the editor to put it in writing. If the editor fails to send you a confirming letter, *you* can send one—but, again, when the stakes are really high (for example, where a book is involved), don't do this kind of thing without professional help.

For most periodical contributions, you can send a polite letter, something along the following lines: "This will confirm our telephone discussion of this morning in which you advised me that payment for my article would be $250, payable within thirty days after you accept the final draft for publication." This works—but bear in mind that "acceptance" can mean different things to different publishers. For some, acceptance is the day the manuscript arrives in a form they can use; for others, it is after the publisher returns from his round-the-world cruise and gets around to reading the mail that has accumulated on his desk.

A book contract is governed by custom of the trade as much as by law. Its basic terms may vary, depending on the kind of book involved—college textbook, elementary or high school textbook (called "el-hi" in the trade), school and library edition, trade publication, or mass-market edition. There are three important things to remember about all book contracts, however:

- The publisher should pay you and not the other way around.
- All book contracts are negotiable, at least to some extent.
- There is no such thing as an industry-standard book contract.

Even though there is no industry-standard book contract, there are several clauses that you can expect to find, in some form or another, in every one of them. These include the *delivery clause* (specifying when you will turn in the book, how long it will be, and what it will cover) and the *warranty clause* (in which you warrant that the work is your own and doesn't infringe on the rights of anyone else). There is also usually an *indemnity clause* in which you agree to indemnify the publisher if you breach the warranty clause.

A book contract also normally includes a *copyright clause*, in which it notes who will hold the copyright in the work and, often, the form of the copyright notice that will appear in the work; in addition, this clause normally specifies whose obligation it is to register the work with the Copyright Office.

Closely related is the *grant of rights*, which states which rights in the work you are granting to the publisher. This is usually broken down into the book rights granted (hardcover or paperback, English or another language, in the United States or throughout the world) and the subsidiary rights (foreign sales and foreign language rights, serial and condensation rights, book club rights, film, electronic, and audio rights, and merchandising rights).

Sometimes these clauses contradict each other, saying, for example, that the author "retains the copyright" but "grants all rights" to the publisher. Such a contract should, by all means, be modified, restricting the grant to those rights that the author is willing to give up and that the publisher is capable of exploiting. (A small press with no subsidiary rights department or experience may not have a clue as to how to sell movie or serial or foreign rights.)

A grant of rights is a grant of control; the party holding those rights is the one who may market them. It should be noted, however, that controlling the rights does not mean keeping all of the money for them; most reasonable book contracts provide that the author and the publisher split the proceeds from the sale of subsidiary rights, although the percentages may vary not only from publisher to publisher but also from one right to another.

There are often several sections regarding *compensation*. If an advance is to be paid, the contract should state how much and when (whether on signing, on acceptance, or on publication, or a combination of these dates); it should state the royalties such payments are to be advanced against (an advance must be earned back out of the percentage of sales to which the writer is entitled); and it should state the intervals at which royalties will be paid once the advance has been earned back.

Closely allied are schedules defining how subsidiary rights sales will be divided—how much of the money received from a foreign publisher, filmmaker, or other subsidiary rights licensee will go to the publisher, and how much to the author, and when the author's share of such earnings will be paid over. Other clauses note how many free copies the author will receive and what discount he or she can have on the purchase of additional copies. Some publishers restrict the author from the direct sale of such copies; others don't seem to mind and even encourage it.

Among the other clauses that should be contained in a publishing contract are the *termination clause*—the clause that allows the publisher or the author to end their relationship, especially if one or the other has failed to deliver as agreed in the contract—and the *out-of-print clause,* which allows the author to take back the publication rights if the publisher fails to keep the book in print.

Contracts may, of course, contain other provisions, and each publisher will word its contract clauses differently. The writer can usually negotiate changes in the wording of various clauses and add clauses of his or her own. A book contract defines the scope of the publisher's and author's interests in the copyright in the work, and it should cover all the rights in the work, including the right to prepare derivative works such as sequels and films.

Drafting or negotiating a publishing contract is not a job for an amateur. If you think your work has any lasting value—and if someone is willing to pay you for the privilege of publishing it, it probably does—be careful what rights you give away. Get help in interpreting the contract and negotiating its terms, and don't sign it if you aren't comfortable with what it contains. When you put your name on a document, you are signifying that you have read it, understand its contents, and agree to be bound by it. Keep that in mind before you sign.

14.

Moral Rights

Assignment letters and book contracts do not always specify how much editing of a work will be permitted, or even whether you will get to review galleys before the work sees print. In many foreign countries, you may have the "moral right" to object to changes in your manuscript even without a contract saying so.

Moral rights fall into two categories, those affecting a work's attribution, and those affecting its integrity. The right of attribution is the right to have your name on a piece you have written, or to remove your name from a piece that is so altered that you no longer feel it is your work. (The terminology, like the right, originated in France, where it is generally termed the right to "paternity.") The right of integrity is the right to have the work appear substantially as you wrote it, without any changes that might distort its meaning or your style.

The U.S. Copyright Law is intentionally silent regarding these rights. When the United States joined the Berne Convention, which contains a moral rights provision in its text,

Congress sidestepped the issue by stating categorically that ratification of the Berne does not "expand or reduce any right of an author . . . to claim authorship in a work; or to object to any distortion, mutilation, or other modification of, or other derogatory action in relation to, the work, that would prejudice the author's honor or reputation."

As with any law, there are likely to be challenges to the constitutionality of parts of the Berne Convention Implementation Act, as well as variations in its interpretation in different jurisdictions. It is altogether possible that, someday, a court may hold that the United States could not adopt the Berne Convention without also adopting its moral rights provisions. This may wreak havoc with what publishers have long felt to be their prerogative: the right to edit a piece as they please.

Under the Berne Convention, the moral right of authors in the integrity of their work is considered *inalienable*—it cannot be assigned, and survives even the sale of a work of art or the assignment of copyright. This is not generally true in the United States except for paintings, photographs, drawings, prints, or sculptures reproduced in no more than two hundred signed and numbered copies. Some states, like New York and California, also have laws that protect works of "fine art" (writing is not included in this definition) from mutilation by later owners.

Although this area of the law is developing and changing in the United States as a result of authors' increased knowledge and awareness, currently these rights that Congress neither expanded nor reduced must be found in statutes and cases dealing with other areas of law besides copyright.

One of these is contract law. Because moral rights are not recognized as inalienable in the United States, it is possible to sign them away—often as part of an all-rights assignment.

In the past, an all-rights assignment was considered the equivalent of an assignment of copyright, but since a U.S. copyright does not include moral rights, an all-rights assignment may now be the broader term, incorporating an author's moral rights where an assignment of copyright does not.

Check your contract. Did you authorize editorial changes, such as "ordinary copyediting," or does the contract expressly note that "no changes may be made without the consent of the author"? If there is no reference to editorial changes, and if you did not sign away all rights or the copyright, you may have remedies available to you for gross, unauthorized changes.

One such remedy may be found in the derivative rights section of the U.S. Copyright Law; you own the exclusive right to prepare derivative works based on your copyrighted works until you sign that right away. An article that began as yours but is utterly distorted could be construed as a derivative work, and if the distortion is *unauthorized,* you may have grounds for a copyright infringement action.

If the changes are so drastic that they have damaged your reputation, you may have recourse under libel law. Your recovery may depend on a number of factors, including whether the changes have actually damaged—rather than improved—your text, whether you have a provable reputation (either as a writer or as an expert in some field), and the number of people who know of you who are likely to have seen the altered piece with your name on it.

But what if the problem isn't that your name or pseudonym has appeared *on* a story, but that it was left *off?* This is part of the "attribution" aspect of moral right. Until that right exists in the United States, your remedy may lie in trademark law, specifically the portion that prohibits anyone from "reverse passing off"—that is, putting his or her name on the work of another.

While it might be possible to recover damages under any of these theories of law, an ounce of prevention can be worth pounds of legal remedy. A written agreement that allows you to review the galleys enables you to protest alterations before they find their way into print.

15.

Collaboration Agreements

In addition to contracts with publishers and agents, the relationship between two or more writers working together, and the one between author and subject in a ghostwriting situation, should also be cemented with a written agreement. How, for example, do you settle the argument of "It was my idea, my outline, my characters" as opposed to "I did virtually all of the actual writing"? How do you weigh someone's life-story rights against the effort of organizing them into a coherent memoir, especially if the subject will be taking all the credit for the book? A written contract is also a good idea when you are interviewing someone and want to make sure no one will have access to the same material and be able to write a competing article or steal your thunder before your book comes out.

Drafting a collaboration or ghostwriting agreement requires an understanding not only of copyright law, but also of the publishing and television and film industries, because if you don't know what a publisher or production company will expect from you, you won't know how to divvy up the responsibilities—not to mention that you may be expecting rewards that are unlikely, if not impossible. An agreement need not be formal; it can even take the form of a letter or memo signed by both parties. Remember, however, that the simpler the document appears on its face, the more care must be taken in drafting it, so find yourself an attorney who is experienced in such matters and knows the customs prevalent in these industries. Although drafting such an agreement is not something you should do yourself, you can keep your costs down if you can bring your lawyer a fairly detailed description of what you want in the agreement.

What follows is a brief outline of some of the points to be covered in such an agreement. If you and your cowriter or subject find yourselves unable to come to an accommodation regarding these basic points, consider the fact that no matter how great the idea is, maybe you shouldn't be working together in the first place.

- *Determine whose story it is.* If your "partner" merely came up with an idea, but you fleshed it out and did all of the writing, it is likely that he or she has no copyrightable interest. If, however, you rashly offered at the onset to split the proceeds fifty-fifty, you may be bound by an oral contract to do just that. In the end, if you're having second thoughts and the two of you can come to other terms that seem more equitable, be sure to firm them up in writing to avoid any possibility of being held to your original deal. Have this agreement drawn up for you by an attorney to be sure it cancels any obligations you might have previously committed to.
- *Confirm your general understanding.* What do you intend that each of you will contribute? Knowing this can help

you determine what portions of the project each of you will control. Will one of you be responsible for the research and organization while the other prepares the text? Will you each write alternate chapters? Will each of you be responsible for the development of a different character? If so, say so.

• *Decide what each of you will control.* When you are writing another person's life story, you may want to give the subject the last word on what will be included or left out (subject, of course, to libel considerations) while you, as the writer, have the final say on grammar. Individuals normally own the rights to their life stories, unless these stories have been reported so widely that they've fallen into the public domain. But if the story has not become public property and you want the *exclusive* rights to tell it, you need to say so in your contract; otherwise there is nothing to stop your subject from giving an interview— or the whole story—to someone else.

When entering into a ghostwriting contract with someone you do not know well, it is always a good idea to ask whether your subject has entered into similar agreements in the past; you might be writer number three or four in a sequence of collaborators! You should make sure none of them still possesses a continuing legal interest in the subject's story.

• *Determine how far your rights extend.* If you are writing a book based on someone else's life story, does your agreement prevent anyone else from buying movie rights or doing a magazine interview? If not, you need to assess whether a prepublication magazine interview would help promote the book or would steal your thunder. Discuss this with your subject, and decide whether foreclosing any interviews until after the book is published is in your best interests; if so, add that prohibition to the contract.

You should also come to an agreement as to what share of movie or article rights each of you will receive. Remember when deciding this that control over these rights, or compensation for selling them, need not be split evenly, if at all. The key is to settle on whatever works for you, and then cement it in writing.

- *Come to an agreement regarding copyright ownership.* Any time two or more people share a copyright, any one of them can sign a nonexclusive contract for publication, although signatures of all copyright holders are necessary for an exclusive contract. Any of you can produce a sequel (subject to paying over the appropriate portion of the profits to the others). And any of you can use or authorize the use of your characters in another work or in merchandise.

  Because of this, you may want to agree from the start that while you are all alive and competent, none of you will publish a derivative work or authorize any exploitation of the work without the consent of all (or a majority, if there are many) of the others. Keep in mind the fact that if a collaborator dies, you'll be dealing with heirs who have inherited his or her rights. You cannot always bind heirs, but even so, you may want to provide by agreement among the collaborators that the surviving creator will control all rights during his or her lifetime, so long as the heirs receive their share of the proceeds. At least, with such an agreement, you have a horse race.

- *Protect your interests in the event that your collaborator abandons the project.* If your coauthor loses interest, will you have the right to finish the work alone? If you and your subject have a falling out after you've spent the better part of a year transcribing interviews and preparing a first draft, will you be reimbursed for your time and effort—even if another writer replaces you?

The agreement can provide that the party leaving the project will agree to abandon all interest in it, but—for having participated at all—perhaps the departing party should be entitled to receive a small financial share of the proceeds. The amount of that share can be determined up front or decided upon when that party leaves the project.

• *Decide who will be responsible if something goes wrong.* A publisher will normally require all parties who are collectively termed "the author" to warrant that the book is original, does not infringe on anyone else's copyright, and doesn't defame anyone, so you could be jointly responsible for damages resulting from breach of this warranty. This means you could wind up paying for something your writing partner has done, unless your agreements with each other—and with the publisher—provide otherwise.

Under this clause, defamation can prove of special importance to anyone writing someone else's life story. If, in telling you his or her story, your subject plays fast and loose with the truth, or merely slants it a bit, and a lawsuit results, are you going to wind up paying? Although a paragraph in your agreement stating that your subject will assume all liability for defamation may not provide complete legal protection, it should at least provide you with a basis for defense.

• *Consider the effect of circumstances beyond your control.* What if the publisher wants the finished book within six months and your partner slips on the stairs and spends those six months in a coma? If, as a consequence, you find yourself writing the entire book, should the split of profits and copyright still be the same as if your partner had pulled his or her weight? You can provide for such contingencies by agreeing that the percentages each party will receive will be adjusted if their contributions substantially depart from what was originally anticipated. (This is another reason for stating your general understanding, so that you know just what it was that you originally anticipated each party's contribution would be!)

• *Determine each party's fiscal liability.* What if your partner is an artist or photographer who fails to contribute his or her share of the book and you have to pay out of pocket for someone else to do so? What if you can't complete the work by yourself and the publisher demands the advance back? If your partner's share has been spent, the publisher could come after you for the entire amount, even though you received only half.

In addition to whatever you work out with your writing partner, your best protection from liability for your collaborator's failings, whether intentional or accidental, is to adjust your agreement with the publisher so that it separates your accountability. In case your publisher balks at such a provision, make sure your collaboration agreement includes a stipulation that each of you will repay the other for any losses resulting from your personal acts or omissions relating to the contract.

• *Determine an equitable division of the proceeds.* If there are two of you, is fifty-fifty a split that fairly reflects the contribution each of you is making? You can settle on different percentages, but make sure you set that out in your contract.

You should also be clear on reimbursement of out-of-pocket expenses. Is one of you laying out a lot of money up front for typing, copying, faxing, legal fees, long-distance telephone calls, or permission to use quoted material or photographs? If you mean for this to be reimbursed before the rest of the money is divided, say so now to avoid battles later. Be sure, too, to define which out-of-pocket expenses will be reimbursed, or you may find yourself paying for your collaborator's new computer or "research" cruise.

Consider, too, that there are creative ways of splitting an advance, depending on responsibility and need. If half the advance is to be paid on signing and the other half on acceptance, and one of you needs the money to live on while writing the book but the other has outside income, the on-signing check could go to the first and the on-acceptance check to the other. In some ghosting situations, the writer might receive all of the advance, while the subject receives all royalty payments until the score is even (after which royalties will be split between them).

- *Decide how the byline will read.* Unless you and your coauthor are writing under a single pseudonym, someone's name will have to go first. In some fields, it may be important to be "first author" when job evaluations come around. For the rest of us, this may merely be a function of ego—or of "justice." If this is settled up front, you may avoid a knockdown, drag-out fight that keeps a finished project from being published—but if you can't decide on the byline, how are you going to decide where to put the commas in the text?

Where your name goes when you're writing someone else's story, or whether your byline appears at all, depends on the circumstances of the collaboration. Many celebrities prefer to pretend they've done all of the writing on "their" book themselves. If they're paying you big money to write the book, this may be all right—but when you're working with a local subject, you may both be working "on spec" in the hope of a sale that may never materialize. If it finally does, at the very least you will probably want the credit.

The style you choose is up to the two of you; alternatives include "by John Doe *as told to* Richard Roe," "by John Doe *with* Richard Roe," and "by John Doe *and* Richard Roe."

- *What if there are more than two of you?* Where there is no contract and there appear to be a number of partners involved in a project, courts will generally assume that each of you is entitled to an equal share. If you're bringing in another participant for just a small portion of the book, such as the sidebars or pie charts, you might want a contract among the three of you that clarifies that the third person does not own an equal share.

  Remember that *any* share of the copyright—even 1 percent—entitles an author to exercise all of the exclusive rights of a copyright holder, including authorizing publication or preparing derivative works, so while giving your new associate a share of the proceeds, it should be made clear from the outset, in writing, that he or she has no claim on the copyright.

All of these things should be discussed openly and frankly before you embark on any collaboration. Knowing just where you stand will go a long way toward creating a smoother working relationship.

16.

The Global Village and the Information Superhighway

As I mentioned in chapter 1, this book is about *U.S.* copyright law. However, the expansion of international electronic communications and the development of the global marketplace have made the copyright laws of other countries more and more relevant to American writers.

Because most other countries are signatory to the Berne Convention or have ratified the GATT (making them members of the World Trade Organization) or both, and most of the remaining countries have entered into bilateral treaties with the United States, the United States is bound to respect rights of foreign copyright holders, and their governments are technically bound to protect U.S. copyrights. How far that protection goes depends on the nation involved. In some countries the rules are not only more comprehensive but also more strictly enforced; other countries may pay only lip service to copyright protection. The important thing to remember is that what holds true of copyright law in one country may not hold true in others.

To a certain extent, the multilateral treaties and conventions hold all signatory states to certain minimum standards. Under the Berne Convention, for example, a country may not require the citizens of any other Berne country to comply with formalities in order to preserve their copyrights. That was why our notice requirement had to be scrapped when the United States joined the Berne. However, the Berne Convention cannot govern what a country requires of its own citizens—which is why those holding copyrights in U.S. works must still register their copyrights before bringing infringement suits, although those holding copyrights in Berne works whose country of origin is *not* the United States need not do so.

Canada and the United States—though they share the same continent, a common language, and a common legal heritage— are a good example of how copyright laws of neighboring countries can differ. In both countries the term of copyright is currently the life of the author plus seventy years, but in Canada this is the case for all works that haven't fallen into the public domain, while in the United States, because changes in the law were not made retroactive, we have that multitiered term of copyright I described in chapter 5.

In the United States, works of the federal government are automatically in the public domain; however, in Canada, works of the Canadian government *are protected* as "Crown copyright," and the Canadian government is vigorous in its prosecution of infringers. And while Canada has no equivalent to the American freelance or work-for-hire provisions, when a photographic portrait is commissioned in Canada, the copyright belongs to the commissioning party—whereas in the United States, as with any other copyrightable work, the copyright belongs to the photographer unless the photographer assigns the copyright or the work qualifies as a work made for hire.

Even more confusing, especially in view of the North American Free Trade Agreement, is the fact that both Canada and Mexico have moral rights provisions in their copyright laws, but the United States does not. The Canadian and Mexican provisions differ, however, in that while no artist in either country can assign his or her moral rights, Canadian artists can waive them but Mexican artists and writers retain their moral rights throughout the term of copyright, and no advance waiver is binding on them.

Things become even more complex when you leave the Western Hemisphere. European Union artists generally have moral rights in their works, and the term of copyright in European countries is generally the life of the author plus seventy years. It was largely as a consequence of this longer term—a relatively recent development that has been spreading rapidly—that the United States passed the Sonny Bono Copyright Term Extension Act. There are two reasons for this; the first is that if the multinational conventions to which the United States belongs change their minimum standards, the United States needs to amend its laws to accommodate those standards.

The second reason is closely akin to the reason the United States has signed these accords in the first place. So much of American foreign trade depends on the sale of U.S. copyrighted works, such as movies, music, and computer programs, that the United States must take an active stance to protect the interests of American copyright owners or suffer in the international marketplace. The United States therefore goes out of its way, as a matter of public policy, to be a leader in the area of protection and enforcement of intellectual property rights so that it can, by its own example, justify pressure brought to bear on other countries that do not do so.

Among the reasons the United States joined the Berne Convention (and the World Trade Organization, which was created when the requisite number of countries ratified the GATT) was to stem foreign piracy of U.S. copyrighted works. These international agreements have been only partially successful in that respect, and a number of U.S. trading partners frequently appear on the U.S. Trade Representative's list of less-than-cooperative countries. Unfortunately, it's hard to bring effective sanctions for copyright piracy against a country that might contain a much needed military staging area or strategic oil supplies. In addition, copyright enforcement tends to take second place to antidrug initiatives or the war on terrorism.

But international copyright piracy has the potential for becoming an even more serious problem as the electronic superhighway grows. One of the ways in which writers make money is by retaining as many rights as possible and then reselling their articles over and over to different periodicals. However, when a newspaper or magazine to whom you have sold your work publishes electronically—and the article is thus available on the Internet—subsequent sales may at the least be less profitable, and may even be precluded, depending on how many people log on rather than purchase traditional publications.

When does a newspaper or magazine have the right to publish your work electronically? As noted earlier, some publications have begun claiming that right as a condition of publication; others actually purchase the electronic rights, although the sale price may be a pittance. The Authors Guild and the American Society of Journalists and Authors have strongly suggested that their members not include electronic rights when they sell print rights, or, when they feel they must do so, that they limit the time period during which the grant may be exercised. (There may come a time when a log of website hits—how many people access each work—is used to determine royalties, but that time is not here yet.)

There are several ways in which an author's work finds its way onto the Internet. Sometimes the author, himself or herself, uploads it onto a bulletin board or home page. Sometimes a periodical to which print rights were sold authorizes the text on its pages for electronic publication as well. Sometimes a reader who has found a piece of interest but is not aware of copyright prohibitions will upload the piece in much the same way as he or she would cut out an interesting article or cartoon and send it to a friend. And sometimes someone feeling an obligation to create an archive will decide to upload or store (and make available to others) text that has appeared on the Internet for any of the foregoing reasons.

All of these examples boil down to reprints, and infringe the copyright owner's right to reproduce and distribute a copyrighted work, as well as the display right. Electronic rights are becoming a hot area of copyright—witness the MP3 and Napster cases—but the answers to some of the questions that occur seem fairly clear under a commonsense extrapolation of current copyright law. The answers to other questions, such as allotting compensation, are less clear, however, and may become even more complicated as customary author/publisher agreements evolve to meet the needs of new technology.

Under current law, it seems clear that what rights a publisher has in relation to a contributor depend on the status of the writer. Is the piece written by a staffer as part of his or her job? If so, it is legally classified as a work made for hire, and the publisher owns all the rights to it and may publish or distribute it as it chooses. Where a piece is written outside the scope of employment—for example, a humorous column written by a copy editor—such articles, like pieces contributed by freelancers, are works in which all rights (including reprint and electronic rights) originate and remain with the author.

Where a work is not a work made for hire, and the grant of electronic rights is not clear, the *Tasini* case, mentioned earlier (see page 39), may lend some clarity. Because the drafters of the current U.S. copyright law understood that many newspapers and magazines do not habitually use contracts, they built in a special section of the law to address the rights of authors in their contributions to collective works. I've mentioned it before. It reads as follows:

> Copyright in each separate contribution to a collective work is distinct from copyright in the collective work as a whole, and vests initially in the author of the contribution. In the absence of an express transfer of the copyright or of any rights under it, the owner of copyright in the collective work is presumed to have acquired only the privilege of reproducing and distributing the contribution as part of that particular collective work, any revision of that collective work, and any later collective work in the same series [§ 201 (c)].

The first sentence of this section of the law is pretty clear: Copyright—the right to reproduce a work, distribute it, display it, perform it, and create derivative works based on it—initially belongs to the creator of the work. When a publication offers to supply reprints, either in hard copy or online or by authorizing others (such as a reprint service) to do so, this infringes the author's copyright.

The second sentence of that section of the law, although its construction seems to imply a restrictive reading ("acquired *only* the privilege of . . ."), contained a certain amount of ambiguity until the Supreme Court clarified it in *Tasini*. A revision of a collective work or a later collective work in the same series does not include an electronic version.

The best way of settling the issue of electronic rights—or any rights, for that matter—is through a written agreement. However, although such an agreement can protect your works from unauthorized exploitation by your publisher, it won't help much in dealing with the international distribution of your copyrighted material by an admiring fan who thought he or she was doing you a favor, or with a teenager obsessed with the idea that everything should be on the Internet and all of it should be free! The best you can do under those circumstances, if you can actually find the miscreant to sue, is to have registered your work in a timely fashion so that you can win the largest amount with the smallest hassle—and garner reimbursement of your attorney's fees while doing so.

17.

Some Other Avenues of Protection

In addition to the protection that a contract may provide, you can protect your work product through copyright registration before submission, but this is not normally necessary in the literary world; most publications find it more expedient to edit your work to suit their needs than to assign someone else to duplicate your efforts. Registration before publication will allow you faster access to the courts in the event of out-and-out piracy, but such instances are rare in the publishing industry. And since there is no *copyright* protection for an idea, merely for the way in which you have expressed that idea, registration before submission will not be of much use if your article is rejected and another on the same subject appears.

Ideas for writing projects can sometimes be protected under other theories of law, such as unfair competition or unjust enrichment. Unfortunately, it may be difficult to establish the proof necessary to sustain such a case. The simplest way to protect your ideas for your writing may be to keep them confidential until the project has been completed.

Another way to establish such protection is through a non-disclosure agreement—one that binds the person or company to whom you are submitting your idea (and any of their employees) not to disclose the material to anyone. Such agreements are more widely used in the computer industry than in the literary world, and you will probably find them difficult to obtain unless you have considerable clout. What you are more likely to encounter, especially in the music and film industries, is a requirement that *you* sign a document releasing the producer from any liability if material similar to yours is already in development.

There are a lot of myths that circulate among writers regarding what their rights are in their works and how to preserve those rights. For example, writers often ask me if they should mail their materials to themselves. This practice, known sometimes as a "poor man's copyright," does *not* afford copyright protection. It is, however, an effective way to prove that the work in question existed, and was in your possession, as of the mailing date.

Such proof may be of use in a dispute over whether you or someone else who was privy to your work actually created it. Since the postmark proves that you possessed the manuscript on the day the letter was mailed, it may establish that you had it first. But to be of any evidentiary value, the envelope must remain sealed until the matter goes to court and the judge orders it opened. Certified mail, with the stubs of the return receipt providing a seal, is even better for this purpose, provided you save the return receipt.

Remember, however, that there is no copyright protection when someone spontaneously develops material virtually identical to yours. In order to successfully prosecute for infringement you normally must prove that the alleged infringer had access to your work. This is the reason for keeping copies of your correspondence—both submission letters and rejection slips. You might also want to keep a copy of the masthead of a publication to which you have submitted your work in order to document the individuals who are likely to have seen the submission.

I've mentioned that there is no copyright in an idea, but when you pitch a story to the movies, the idea is often precisely what you are trying to sell. You pitch ideas—in the most concise form you can—to film producers, who, if they like them, ask to see "treatments." A treatment is a summary of the way you propose to develop your script but, because movies and television programs are normally collaborative efforts, the final form of the script often bears little resemblance to the treatment.

Still, if yours was the germ that sparked the project, how can you protect your idea? The answer may lie in protections offered to its members by the screenwriters' union, the Writers Guild of America. The WGA provides nonmembers as well as members with a registry for scripts and treatments. Registered works are assigned a number that should be placed on the script or treatment before it is offered to a producer.

Producers who want to deal with WGA members (or members of its sister unions, to which virtually every film professional belongs) must follow WGA's guidelines in paying for stories, treatments, and scripts and in granting screen credit to the authors of those materials. Even if you're not a member (you can't—and don't have to—join until you've sold your first script to a union producer), you have the tacit clout of the WGA behind you in these matters.

You can register a script or even a novel or collection of poems with the Writers Guild of America, West, Inc., 7000 W.

3rd Street, Los Angeles, California 90048–4329 (online at www.wga.org), if you are west of the Mississippi, or with the Writers Guild of America, East, Inc., 555 West 57th Street, New York, New York 10019, if you are located east of the Mississippi (although if you submit your registration to the wrong WGA, it will not be refused). The current cost for non-members registering up to 150 pages is $22, and must be paid by money order, MasterCard, or Visa—a personal check is *not* acceptable. Registration is good for ten years and can be renewed. For more detailed information, you can call their recorded hotline at (212) 757-4360, or visit them online (www.wgaeast.org).

Registering a script with the WGA is not the same thing as registering it with the Copyright Office, and will not enable you to commence a lawsuit or to recover statutory damages or attorney's fees in that suit. It will provide evidence for a suit, however, and may provide the basis for a later arbitration under the WGA's rules if the idea is pirated.

18.

Hiding Behind an Alias

I've mentioned that copyrights in pseudonymous and anonymous works published after 1978 exist for a time period different from that of works whose authors are acknowledged in print.

Copyrights in works written under a pseudonym (pen name) can be recorded under that pseudonym, and the copyright notice on your pseudonymous work can cite your pseudonym, rather than your real name, as copyright owner. Under the 1976 law, pseudonymous and anonymous works are protected by copyright for ninety-five years from the date of first publication (or 120 years from creation of the work) unless the author is identified.

If you live longer than twenty-five years after the first publication of your pseudonymous work (or any of your works that appeared in print without attribution), you may want to extend the copyright protection to the normal term—your life plus seventy years—by letting the Copyright Office know you are the author. To identify yourself, file a statement with the Copyright Office telling them the name of your pseudonymous or anonymous work, the date it was published, your pseudonym (if any), and your real name and date of birth.

Another way to come out of the closet for copyright purposes is to lay claim to a pseudonymous or anonymous work *when you register it*. You can give your real name as the author of the work on the registration form, adding "writing as _____" or "writing under the pseudonym _____." Of course, with this information on record, your cover will be blown if anyone looks you up in the Copyright Office files, since the files are public records. Whether you keep your name secret or not, don't forget to check off the appropriate boxes on the form when the work you are registering is pseudonymous or anonymous.

Anonymous publication of your work may occur when a publication, either inadvertently or as a matter of editorial policy, omits your byline. But why would you want to write anything under a pseudonym? Probably the most popular reason is to protect your privacy. Writing fiction under a pseudonym allows you to throw off the fetters of inhibition; writing an exposé under an alias can protect you from hate mail and other kinds of retribution.

Pen names are often used by authors who have made their reputations in one area and want to write on a totally unrelated subject—mathematician Charles Dodgson writing children's fantasies as Lewis Carroll comes to mind. A man who wants to write romances or a woman who wants to break into a traditionally "male" field such as action/adventure or hard science fiction may find that using a pseudonym of the opposite sex boosts sales and adds credibility.

Pen names are also useful when you write in different genres because you may develop a different following for each category (such as westerns, science fiction, mystery, or romance) in which you write. Readers devoted to your westerns might be upset were they to purchase one of your books and discover, after they got it home, that it was a romance.

A pseudonym is also a convenient cover when several persons are collaborating on a book, or when different authors contribute books to an established series.

In most states, so long as you don't do so for fraudulent purposes, you may adopt any name you choose—although it is a good idea to avoid using a name that you know belongs to someone else (unless you know it belongs to a *lot* of people, like "John Smith"). Once you have chosen your pseudonym, it is up to you to determine how many people should be let in on the secret—although, depending on the scope of your use, you may be required to register the name if you live and work in a state with a fictitious names recording requirement, like California or New York.

Unfortunately, it is difficult to autograph a book written pseudonymously, or make promotional appearances, without giving away your identity. And as to the problem of cashing your check, the easiest solution is to let your publisher know what your real name is and to require, as a condition of publishing your work, that the publisher keep your secret.

If you don't want the publisher to know who you are, you might consider selling your material through an agent—you can even give the agent the authority to sign publishing contracts on your behalf, though you should authorize only one contract at a time, and that only after you review it. The publisher pays the agent, who subtracts his or her commission and remits the rest to you—in your real name. No one but you and your agent will know who you are.

If you don't have an agent and don't want to reveal your identity to your publisher, you can inform your bank that you are doing business under an alternative name. Although you must give your real social security number whenever a publisher asks for it, in most states, you need never reveal your real identity to anyone else. However, as I noted, some states—notably California and New York—do require the registration of fictitious names when used in business, so you may want to check with a local attorney to see what rules apply to you.

Generally, however, except for informing the bank, the only other person to whom you must reveal your secret is your friendly tax collector: when you file your income taxes, your pseudonym goes in the place on Schedule C (the Statement of Profit and Loss from Business or Profession) that asks for your "business name."

19.

Naming Names—
Libel and Privacy

I am often asked if it is enough to change the names if you want to write about your friends or neighbors. This involves not copyright law, but libel and privacy laws. In the United States, where freedom of the press is guaranteed by the Constitution, there is a fine balancing act between the public's right to know and the individual's right to privacy. Among the factors to be considered in deciding what you can or cannot say in print are the nature of the writing (whether it is fiction or nonfiction), the status of the person you are writing about (whether he or she is a government official, a celebrity, or a private citizen), and the value to the public of the subject matter.

Generally, if you are writing fiction, portraying a living person can get you into trouble because fiction, by its very nature, extrapolates from the truth. The fiction writer creates conversations that never took place and puts thoughts and motives in the mind of the character. When the character is a real person, this kind of license can place him or her in a false light.

Though laws in this area vary from state to state, if the reputation of an identifiable living person is damaged by the fictitious adventures you have given him or her, that person can sue you for what has traditionally been called libel (although the preferred term now is "defamation"). Merely changing the name will not protect you if the person remains recognizable in your fiction.

Even when you stick to the facts, when you write about a named or recognizable private citizen, he or she may have a case against you for invasion of privacy. Generally, private citizens have a right to keep their private lives to themselves, unless there is an overweening social benefit to be gained from telling their story. It is possible to get around this where there has been consent, whether actual or implied, by actions like granting an interview.

Celebrities who have chosen to place themselves in the public eye are also assumed to have granted such permission by seeking renown or notoriety. While you must still be careful to be accurate in your reporting, the law gives you more leeway to reveal the details of the lives of celebrities than it does of private citizens.

It is possible for a private citizen to become a temporary or accidental public figure by winning a prize or by becoming the victim of a crime. In such cases, reporters may be free to reveal more details of a private citizen's life, especially in connection with the incident that brought that person to the public's attention. What is permitted at the time someone becomes newsworthy may not be permitted at a later date, however, and care must still be taken to verify the facts. Note, too, that your state may seal court records and have laws restricting reportage about certain crime victims and even *some* criminals, such as minors; check this out before proceeding with any story that may be sensitive.

Public officials not only have fewer rights to privacy and against defamation than private citizens, they also have fewer rights than other public figures. This is because we endow our public officials with the public trust; hence their activities are subject to a greater scrutiny. When the public interest warrants publication of a story that later proves false, those in the public eye generally need to prove that the writer or publisher acted with *actual malice* (a legal term meaning reckless disregard for the truth or falsity of the statement) before they can prevail in court.

Even if your revelations in print are within the law, and any case brought against you for defamation or invasion of privacy is dismissed, defending a lawsuit can be expensive—and if the case goes against you, the verdict can be astronomical.

This is one of the reasons that most publishing contracts contain a warranty clause whereby the author guarantees that his or her work is not defamatory or invasive of anyone's rights, including the right to privacy. Because both author and publisher are usually jointly liable to an injured party, the publisher may find it expedient to defend a lawsuit—but publishing contracts normally require the author to reimburse the publisher for such expenditures. Where the contract does not, if a suit is sustained because of your intentional disregard for the consequences of your words, or even just plain negligence on your part, chances are that an equitable court will require you to reimburse the publisher anyway.

Note that it is possible to defame a person accidentally. The most common way is by using a person's name in your fiction. When you give a character the name of a living person, even when you didn't know he or she existed, you can be guilty of defamation if the details of your character's life are too close to the life of the real person with the same name. For this reason you should always check carefully to make sure that no one by the name you have selected (or a virtually identical name) lives in the neighborhood you have described, or works at a nearly identical job in the city in which you have placed your story.

It is also possible to libel a *corporation* or other group by injuring its reputation. You can only defame or invade the privacy of a *living person*—the dead have no rights in these areas—but remember that corporations, organizations, and similar entities do not die. Take their names in vain at your own risk.

There *is* a related right that can endure *after* an individual's death: the right of publicity. This is the right to use a person's name or image for commercial purposes, and includes use not only in product endorsements and commercials, but also on commercial goods such as calendars or T-shirts. Generally, if the right was exploited during a person's lifetime, it belongs to his or her heirs after death.

The right of publicity has been based traditionally in state, rather than federal, law, but recent rulings have suggested that it may be founded in federal trademark law as well. While every state may not have individual laws or precedents protecting the right of publicity, and while such laws may differ in scope from state to state when they do exist, it is probably safest to assume that commercial use of a person's name or image is protected until proven otherwise.

Indeed, recent cases have held that even the use of celebrity look-alikes and sound-alikes can infringe on the right of publicity and on the derivative right under copyright. Incorporate

20.

Does Crime Pay After All?

When a crime is particularly sensational, books and movies about it often sell well. Because of this, writers often scurry to cover all the details—the gorier, the better. But writing about crimes can cause problems for writers in a number of areas.

As I mentioned in chapter 19, some states have laws forbidding the identification of certain crime victims in print. Identities of minors and victims of "sensitive" crimes, such as rape and incest, may be protected, as may be certain witnesses and undercover police or other government operatives. Some of these restrictions have been found to be unconstitutional, especially where the names in question are part of the public record, but in many places, local custom and courtesy may restrict the publication of some names where the law does not.

Law enforcement agencies sometimes attempt to place restrictions on how many details of a crime may be revealed print. Sometimes this is done with good reason. Although First Amendment guarantee of freedom of the press may nit use of such information in print, an overzealous reporter

20.

Does Crime Pay After All?

When a crime is particularly sensational, books and movies about it often sell well. Because of this, writers often scurry to cover all the details—the gorier, the better. But writing about crimes can cause problems for writers in a number of areas.

As I mentioned in chapter 19, some states have laws forbidding the identification of certain crime victims in print. Identities of minors and victims of "sensitive" crimes, such as rape and incest, may be protected, as may be certain witnesses and undercover police or other government operatives. Some of these restrictions have been found to be unconstitutional, especially where the names in question are part of the public record, but in many places, local custom and courtesy may restrict the publication of some names where the law does not.

Law enforcement agencies sometimes attempt to place restrictions on how many details of a crime may be revealed in print. Sometimes this is done with good reason. Although the First Amendment guarantee of freedom of the press may permit use of such information in print, an overzealous reporter someone else's name, image, or style into your work at your own risk. Check with an attorney if you have doubts about how far you can go.

One further caveat: you can get into serious legal trouble by including edited material within quotation marks. Although most of us hem and haw when we speak and probably wouldn't object to an interviewer correcting an obvious slip of the tongue, such corrections constitute paraphrase rather than quotation. Save the quotation marks for direct quotes—and save your notes and tapes to prove what was actually said. Doing so could save you a bundle in legal defense costs.

who reveals too much can sometimes hamper an ongoing investigation and may even destroy any chance for a conviction because of the effect of widespread pretrial publicity on potential jurors. It is often difficult to balance the public's right to know about a crime against the right of the accused to a fair trial; both rights are protected by the Constitution. A case-by-case determination, with legal assistance where the answer is unclear, is required.

Problems also arise when referring, before trial, to those arrested for crimes. Under the American legal system, a person accused of a crime is presumed to be innocent until proven guilty. Because of this, and to avoid the possibility of defamation, reference should always be made to "alleged" perpetrators and "the accused" rather than to "the criminal" or "the killer." Even after a conviction, there may be restrictions on the publication of a criminal's name—for example, when the criminal has, perhaps as recompense for testimony against associates, come under a witness protection program or, in some jurisdictions, when he or she is a minor.

Of course, there are some convicted criminals who *want* their stories told or to see their names and pictures in the paper. This creates an ethical as well as a legal dilemma: does the public's right to know extend to the point of granting a forum to those who use crime to gain publicity for themselves or their causes? When writers are too quick to cooperate with such persons, they risk aiding and abetting them.

Writing about a crime after conviction can also lead to problems that arise when writers agree to pay fees to, or share royalties with, a criminal. Such agreements are occasioned because while anyone can amass facts that are part of the public record and put them together in a book, books sell better if they contain exclusive, never-before-revealed material.

Sometimes those accused or convicted of crimes may be willing to give you this kind of information just for the publicity or the chance to get their side of the story out to the public; others won't talk unless they are compensated.

Most states have laws preventing criminals from profiting from their crimes—indeed, there are even laws allowing the government to confiscate money paid to others (for example, the criminal's lawyers) if it came from tainted sources (such as drug sales) or to confiscate items purchased with such tainted funds. However, this does not affect the money earned by a nonparticipant who writes about crimes committed by others; one instance in which the shares of the publisher and ghost-writer *were* attached was later reversed on appeal.

The First Amendment to the U.S. Constitution protects the right to earn money from *writing* about crimes, as opposed to earning it from committing them, but this was not always the case. Because of public outrage over convicted criminals earning substantial sums from telling their stories, a number of states and the federal government enacted so-called Son of Sam laws (named for a New York serial killer), which essentially confiscated such earnings.

Money criminals earned from telling their stories remained subject to confiscation until 1991, when the U.S. Supreme Court struck down New York's Son of Sam law—and consequentially most, if not all, of the others then existing throughout the United States. The Court pointed out that confiscating the proceeds of any writing that contained mention of any crime committed by the author was likely to inhibit freedom of speech.

Various state legislatures immediately began looking at ways to get around this, such as lifting the statute of limitations for suing for damages resulting from criminal acts. This would mean that no matter when a criminal came into money, those injured by the crime would not be barred from bringing suit by the passage of time. At present, many victims or their families file civil actions early on, so that a judgment will be on record. A civil judgment against any person generally permits the attachment of any assets that person possesses at the time the judgment is entered or acquires in the future until the amount of the judgment is satisfied.

When your subject is a convicted criminal whose assets are attached, paying for an interview or granting a percentage of your royalties from a book or screenplay to him or her can cause problems when the royalty check arrives.

The determination of just what monies are to be forfeited, and by whom, could even result in litigation. A carefully drafted contract can minimize bookkeeping headaches for a coauthor.

However, other problems have been known to arise from the contract between author and subject. Though such contracts are always a good idea where exclusivity of information is required, they can backfire where criminal subjects—indeed, any subjects—decide you have breached your contract to reveal "the truth" about their cases. You could even find yourself facing a suit for defamation if a disgruntled subject who thought you were going to be sympathetic to his or her cause decides you weren't sympathetic enough. Keep in mind that though there may be honor among thieves, there is not always accord between criminals and their chroniclers.

21.

Arms Against
a Sea of Troubles

I am always amazed at how many writers jump feet first into situations where a person with a modicum of common sense would ordinarily fear to venture. People who haven't visited their doctor in a decade take it upon themselves to write medical advice. Someone who hasn't seen a movie in years will decide to become a film critic. Once a man who had bought and sold a single house came into my office to discuss writing a book based on his experience—a "how-to" book, *not* a humorous reminiscence. And I know of a woman with no legal training who misunderstood some misinformation given to her by an editor and used it as the basis for an error-filled article on copyright law.

To put it bluntly, writing is not always just a matter of putting pen to paper. It may be, if you are writing a humorous anecdote—but not if the anecdote is told at the expense of someone who might sue you for libel or invasion of privacy. If you are writing to convey information, you will need to be sure you have your facts right—and this is especially true in writing the "how-to" piece.

From a legal standpoint, there are innumerable wrong ways to write the "how-to" article, and only two right ways. One of these right ways is to expound on your own expertise in the article, provided that you are, indeed, an expert on a subject. But when you do this, make sure that you can review galleys so that some editor doesn't polish up your style and distort your meaning. (Such editorial "assistance" can often be avoided by choosing your words carefully in the first place—don't just dash off an article without double-checking for typos and slips of the tongue or the mind.)

The alternative, if you, yourself, are not an expert, is to locate one or more people who *are,* and use them as resources. If they differ, you can expound on their differences; if they agree, you can quote them wherever what they've told you seems better set off in their own words. But be forewarned: when you incorporate the advice of experts into a "how-to" article, persuade them, if at all possible, to review your finished piece. If you are not an expert in the field, you may have misinterpreted what they said, and the advice you are purveying may be inaccurate.

People seldom wind up in court for giving incorrect advice in print, but to avoid even that possibility and to keep your reputation either as a reliable journalist or as an expert intact, double-check your facts and the implications of what you are saying—both in your initial manuscript and in your galleys.

Occasionally the publication of incorrect information results in a lawsuit brought by someone who relied, to his or her detriment, on the advice in a printed work. Such suits are founded on many different legal theories, among them the general theory that merchandise you purchase should not be harmful to you—an area of law known as "products liability." Products liability cases are more likely to apply to books so designed that they snap shut and break your finger; generally, the presumption regarding advice found in books is that readers assume the responsibility to act reasonably, no matter what the book tells them. Acting reasonably means reading disclaimers and checking out other sources of information on the same subject before going forward.

Nevertheless, there have been cases where publishers have been held responsible for damages resulting as a consequence of information contained in a book, most notably a case in which a chemistry text juxtaposed instructions for two experiments that, if performed near each other, could cause an explosion. They were, it did, and the injured parties sued.

The publishers lost that liability suit, but even where suits for injuries resulting from faulty directions, unhealthy diet programs, or inaccurate advice are won by the defendant or are dismissed, defending them can be costly. The fact that you might be called upon to repay your publisher for such losses should make you wary of giving advice in print unless you have checked your work thoroughly.

The writing field is fraught with other dangers for the unwary. For example, if you are doing a travel piece and you take a photo of the other tourists in your group, you will need to obtain a release before you offer the photo for publication. (If you take a photo of someone under eighteen, you will need a release from that person's parent or legal guardian.) Private citizens who are not attending a public event (whether it is a lecture or a lynching) have a right to their privacy.

Permissions are also needed when your use of quoted material falls outside the scope of the fair use exception. These permissions should always be in writing, and it is a good idea to include wording to the effect that the person granting the permission *has the authority* to make the grant. The permission should also mention any limitations on the use of the quote—for example, a time period, or a number of copies—and the consideration paid, if any.

If you are basing a how-to piece on your own expertise in your business or profession, it may be possible to obtain liability insurance for errors and omissions; your home owner's or renter's insurance probably provides limited copyright and trademark infringement and libel coverage (although it may not cover these things if the damages are incurred in your professional capacity—check the fine print to be sure). Specific libel and other publishers' liability policies may be too expensive for an individual, but your publisher may be willing to add you to its policy (if it has one). Check this out when negotiating for any project for which you might be likely to incur such liability, since the contract will normally require you to indemnify the publisher for damages paid out to third parties.

Even when you can obtain insurance, remember that it is better to treat it as a safety net rather than a protective shield. Always check and double-check all facts and implications in your writing. As in all legal matters, an ounce of prevention can be worth many pounds of cure.

22.

Infringement and Suits

Ownership of a copyright gives you the exclusive right to reproduce your work in copies, publicly distribute those copies, display or perform the work in public, and produce derivative works based on your work. When someone else exercises one of these rights without your permission, generally your copyright is deemed to have been infringed. The law provides remedies for that infringement.

You must seek those remedies in federal court, because since January 1, 1978, all matters concerning copyright in the United States have come under federal jurisdiction. The rules for enforcement are provided in the U.S. Copyright Law and Codes of Civil and Criminal Procedure. Acting on this may seem simple where there is an out-and-out infringement of one of the five basic rights included in copyright—where, for example, someone reprints your article without your permission—but most infringements are more subtle than that.

Because the U.S. court system is dedicated to providing *equity* (fairness) as well as enforcing the letter of the law, there is a vast gray area into which fall many things that *might* be infringement. Within this vast gray area, the determination of infringement in each instance will depend on the facts surrounding the use.

Don't forget that sometimes a seemingly infringing use will be permitted under copyright law. I discussed "fair use" of copyrighted materials in chapter 8. The law also protects a number of other privileged uses, including limited reproduction by libraries or archives and some performances that occur "in the course of face-to-face teaching activities" (see Copyright Office Circular 21 for details)—or as part of a religious service. Some performances specifically designed for the blind or other handicapped persons may also be permitted. In all of these cases, however, a number of preconditions—defined in the law—must be met before the use will qualify as privileged.

Some matters that might seem to be infringements do not come within the scope of copyright law—protection of ideas, titles, and short phrases, for example, or material that has not been fixed in a tangible medium of expression, such as an extemporaneous speech that is not, in some manner, recorded. Taking such material—or material that is in the public domain—and passing it off as your own may not be *infringement* under the U.S. Copyright Law, but it may be a violation of some *other* area of the law, such as plagiarism or trademark regulation.

Where an act is an explicit violation of one of the rights reserved to the copyright owner—where someone reprints your story (a violation of your exclusive right to reproduce and distribute your work), or reads your poem on television (a violation of your performance right), or puts your article up on a computer bulletin board (the display right), or writes a mystery novel using *your* detective (the derivative right)—you have legal recourse.

However, before you rush off to court, which could prove very expensive, you might want to contact the infringing party or parties and point out that you hold the copyright in the work and their use constitutes infringement. Usually they will be apologetic. If so, you have the option—assuming the use is not offensive to you—of accepting their apology and then offering to settle the matter if they pay you a reasonable fee for one-time rights. You might wind up with money in your pocket *and* a new market for your work.

But what if the use is not a blatant infringement? What if the novel just *seems* to have a plot suspiciously close to yours, or the article just seems to have exploited your research without giving you credit? Bearing in mind that there is no copyright in ideas, what can you do?

Your first task is to prove substantial similarity to your work. If the other novel that you feel is infringing on yours shares only the setting of a brownstone block in New York, the similarity is not substantial. If both your novel and the one you feel copied yours chronicle the lives of three sisters living on that block—one a prim teacher, one a secretary who is secretly a madam, and one a power-hungry politician—you may be approaching what nuclear scientists refer to as the "critical mass." If, in each book, the teacher finally finds love and happiness with the boy next door, the secretary becomes a nun, and the politician murders her lover and spends the rest of her life in jail, you may indeed have your substantial similarity.

Still, if one book is written in the third person and the other in the first, if one book is filled with short sentences and the other with flowery phrases, if one book fills 200 pages and the other is four times as long, the similarity may not be all that substantial after all. Then again, if somewhere in the pages of both books you find the same 600-word description, verbatim to the extent that the same misspelling occurs in both, you probably have all the proof you need.

In that last instance, you may not need to prove that the writer copying your work had access. The court will generally assume it from the identical words *and* the identical errors. But without evidence like those matched sections, the other work will have to pass a second test to establish infringement: the author must have had access to your work.

Access is generally easier to prove if your work has been published and widely distributed. The other writer then must prove that he or she *couldn't have had access* in order to defeat the presumption of copying. But what if neither work was published? The law will generally assume that each work was the original creation of its author unless you can prove that the other author had an opportunity to see your manuscript— perhaps he or she was a slush-pile reader at a publishing house to which you once sent the work.

What if your book was self-published and distributed only within your circle of friends? Access can be proved if the other author once bought a copy, and the carbon of the receipt is still in your receipt book. With any circumstances less obvious than that, you must prove "constructive access." How? If the other author sublet the fully furnished apartment of someone who owns your book, and, indeed, the book is still in the apartment, you have probably succeeded in proving access. If the other author's daughter bought a copy, there *might* be access. If the other author's mother-in-law's best friend bought a copy, there is probably *no* access. It all hinges on what a judge or jury finds it reasonable to believe.

Bear in mind that certain circumstances can defeat the presumption of access. If you write an article about your memories of your grandmother's kitchen and it is published in your local free weekly, and a week later another article on the same subject, but by someone else from another part of the country, appears in a nationally distributed monthly magazine, have they stolen your work?

Of course not. Even though your article was published before theirs came out, the author of the national piece would be unlikely to have seen your local article—and even had there been such access, the normal lag time between submissions to monthly magazines and their publication dates is quite lengthy. This means it is probable that the magazine was already edited (and perhaps even typeset) long before your piece appeared.

Obviously, bringing a case for copyright infringement is not a simple matter. Although the law allows anyone to bring a case *pro se*—on his or her own behalf—remember that common wisdom has it that the lawyer who represents himself has a fool for a client; how much more foolish must be the client whose "lawyer" has no legal training and does not know the law. (The lesson here: don't do this without competent help!)

Note, too, that copyright matters must be brought in the federal courts, courts that do not look kindly upon plaintiffs who clutter up their courtrooms with frivolous lawsuits (a *plaintiff* is the person who brings the suit; the *defendant* is the person who is sued). You must have a reasonable basis for bringing your suit and be reasonably able to sustain your arguments, or you could wind up not only losing but also paying the defendant's attorney's fees.

Essential to your proof is documentary evidence—you must be able to prove that you sent the manuscript to the agent whose writer-wife appears to have copied it. Did you keep copies of your correspondence to him? Did you keep his letter declining to represent you? Can you prove what the text of your manuscript looked like at the time? (This is the only reason for mailing a manuscript to yourself, as mentioned in chapter 17—it provides evidence of what the manuscript looked like at the time of mailing. However, if you break the seal on the envelope before you submit it into evidence, it is no longer of any use.)

Before you can initiate a suit for copyright infringement on any work whose country of origin is the United States, you must register the work. Basically, this applies to any work first published in the United States—or any unpublished work if all of its authors habitually reside in or are citizens of the United States. (Remember, I said *basically*—the rules involving first or simultaneous publication outside the United States and joint authorship with non-U.S. citizens or residents are fairly complex. If your work falls into these categories, you'll need to check the copyright law for the rules that apply in your case—something that requires a fair amount of legal expertise.)

Certain remedies can be lost if the infringement occurs before you register, and the need to register before you bring suit can delay the award of others. Expeditious registration is available, but, as I mentioned in chapter 10, it is quite costly.

A civil copyright case must be brought within three years after the claim accrues. But even if you bring a case within that period of time, there is a doctrine known as "laches" that can result in your losing some of your remedies. If you know about an ongoing infringement, and do nothing about it for two years and eleven months, even if you ultimately bring a suit within the time allowed by law, you could lose some of your remedies for failure to act when you first learned of the infringement.

However, the remedies available to a copyright owner who prevails in court comprise a mighty arsenal. If you can prove that someone has infringed your copyright, you may be able to obtain an injunction to stop the infringing acts. If, after an injunction is issued, the infringer continues to distribute the pirated copies of your work or to perform your play, he or she can be held in contempt of court and fined or even jailed.

It is also possible to obtain an order for the impounding of infringing goods and the materials—such as plates, molds, or negatives—used to produce them. The court may order the infringing goods (and the materials used to make them) destroyed or otherwise disposed of. In addition, the court can order the infringer to pay the actual losses incurred by the copyright owner, as well as any profits pocketed by the infringer as a result of the unauthorized use of the work.

If you meet the criteria for timely registration of your work, the court can award statutory damages of anywhere from $200 to $150,000 to you instead of your actual losses and the infringer's profits. The amount is in the court's discretion, depending on what the court "considers just." Among the factors the court considers in determining what is just are whether the infringer "was not aware and had no reason to believe" he or she was infringing, and whether the infringement "was committed willfully." (This is a good reason for making sure a copyright notice appears on your work, even though it is no longer required on works publicly distributed after March 1, 1989. If the notice appears on your work, an infringer cannot argue that he or she did not know the work was protected.)

If you win, the court can also order the other side to pay your attorney's fees—provided you have met the criteria for timely registration. Copyright suits are expensive, and the fees you pay your counsel can exceed the award you receive for the copyright infringement; recovery of attorneys' fees, as well as damages, can thus prevent your victory from being a Pyrrhic one. This is an added incentive to register any of your works that you think might be infringed, and to do so promptly— preferably within the first three months after publication, so that all of your remedies are protected.

Of course, even if you prevail, if a defendant has no money to pay the judgment, you may have to be satisfied with nonmonetary remedies, such as injunction and impounding. There are also instances where the infringing party who appears to have blatantly infringed your work may get off scot-free.

Take the example of a magazine that reprints one of your works without your permission. When you contact the editors, they inform you that they obtained reprint permission from your original publisher.

If the work was first published before January 1, 1978, and there was no contract, the first publisher may well have the right to grant reprint permission, since, under the 1909 law, mere delivery of the manuscript generally was enough to transfer copyright, at least for the first term. And if an old-law work was published prior to 1964 and its copyright wasn't renewed during the twenty-eighth year after its first publication, the work may now be in the public domain, in which case no reprint permission is needed. However, where the work was first published after January 1, 1978, the publisher has only those rights you have granted it (although where there is no contract, a collective work does have the right to republish the piece in its own subsequent editions).

If the work was published before March 1, 1989, and if the only copyright notice printed on it was that of the first publisher, the magazine reprinting it may have a complete defense against your charges of infringement because it obtained reprint permission from the person or company named in the copyright notice. This doesn't mean, however, that you are without a remedy. If the first publisher granted rights it didn't own, *it* is accountable to you for any fees it received for transfers and licenses, and must pay those over to you—although if it granted the permission without charge there's nothing to collect.

There is also nothing in it for you when the Justice Department brings a criminal action against someone who has infringed your work—nothing, that is, but satisfaction. Criminal cases must be instituted by the government, and can only be brought when an infringement is both willful and "for commercial advantage or private financial gain," or by having made or distributed copies with a total retail value of at least $1,000 in a six-month period. A criminal conviction for copyright infringement can carry with it a sentence of—depending upon the specifics of the crime—up to five years and a fine of up to $250,000 for each offense. (This money goes into the government's pockets, not those of the copyright owner.) In addition, a criminal conviction for infringement brings with it the forfeiture and destruction of the infringing articles.

Criminal actions can also be instituted for intentionally placing a fraudulent notice on publicly distributed copies of a work, for fraudulently removing or altering the copyright notice on copyrighted works, and for knowingly putting false information on a copyright application. Conviction for any of these acts carries with it a fine of up to $2,500. Again, this money doesn't go into the pocket of the copyright owner, but there is nothing—outside of the statute of limitations—to stop the copyright owner from bringing a civil suit in addition to the government's criminal action.

23.

Contacting the Copyright Office

The Copyright Office will provide circulars concerning its operations and copies of its forms. Address your letters to:

> Library of Congress
> Copyright Office
> 101 Independence Avenue, S.E.
> Washington, D.C. 20559-6000

Or visit them online (www.copyright.gov). Circulars and fact sheets are also available online (www.copyright.gov/circs/). You will need Form TX (with instructions) or Short Form TX for literary works, Form PA (with instructions) or Short Form PA for works of the performing arts such as plays or scripts, or Form GRCP for group registrations.

Any forms you may need can also be ordered by telephone from the Copyright Hotline, which will record your request twenty-four hours a day. The number is (202) 707-9100. You must know the name and number of the form or kit you are ordering, and give it along with your name and address.

Circulars and forms are free, but the Copyright Office cannot always respond immediately, so don't be surprised if it takes some time for your materials to arrive.

The Copyright Office also has a Public Information Office, which will answer many of your basic questions about copyrights. Call them at (202) 707-3000 (TTY: (202) 707-6737), or visit them on the fourth floor of the Madison Building of the Library of Congress during normal government working hours. (You must first stop at the Reader Registration Station, presenting valid photo identification, to obtain a Reader Identification Card.)

At the new home page on the World Wide Web, you can download forms using Adobe Acrobat Reader® (which may be downloaded for free from Adobe Systems Incorporated through links at that Internet site). You must reproduce the forms as two-sided, 8½- by 11-inch head-to-head copies before attempting to use them. (Short forms are one-sided).

You can also do online searches of Copyright Office registrations filed since 1978 (www.copyright.gov/records). Pre-1978 records must be searched in person at the Copyright Office.

24.

Rules to Live By

Due to changes brought about by United States membership in the Berne Convention, ratification of the GATT and NAFTA, and problems produced by the growth of electronic media, American copyright and publishing law may at first seem more confusing than ever, but most writers will find they can't go wrong by following these simple rules:

1. Whenever possible, have your copyright notice put on your published works, even though it isn't required anymore—it gives you more protection against infringers.
2. Register any work of more than transitory value, and do so preferably within three months of the work's first publication—this will give you access to the strongest sanctions against infringers.
3. Always assume that any work from which you want to quote is covered by copyright unless proven to the contrary—since notice is no longer required, you're not

going to be able to tell if a work is protected without inquiry into its copyright status.

4. Make sure you understand any document you sign, and never sign unless you agree with the terms it contains.

5. Always be sure of your facts before you go to press, and check your material for implications as well.

6. If in doubt about whether you can legally publish anything, check it out with an expert; it's worth the cost if it helps you to avoid liability and litigation, and can be a small price to pay for peace of mind.

Index

About the Author

ELLEN M. KOZAK has practiced copyright, publishing, entertainment, and media law in Milwaukee, Wisconsin, for more than twenty-five years. Her articles have appeared in newspapers and magazines throughout the country, and she is also the author of a pseudonymous series of science fiction novels, as well as the prize-winning book, *From Pen to Print: The Secrets of Getting Published Successfully.*